Becoming the Reel Raphael

KENN SCOTT

Published by Funk Communication Technologies INC

Cover Illustration by Greg Aronowitz
Book design & interior layout by Kevin Vain and Ayesha Knox from
CoLAB Creative Group LLC

Some names have been changed to protect privacy.
This book is printed on paper that's not good for smoking.

ISBN: 978-1-7340518-0-3

DEDICATION

This book is dedicated to my mom and dad;
thanks for giving me a chance.
And to all the dreamers.
Never let the bastards get you down.

ACKNOWLEDGMENTS:

Thank you for reading this book. It was a substantial undertaking for me to get this thing completed. Fortunately, I was blessed to have several capable, talented, and intelligent individuals helping and encouraging me throughout the process. First off, thanks to Ric Meyers; as my authoring sifu, you gave me the confidence and inspiration to complete a book on my own. Thanks to Lynell Bond, Jenny Stewart, Clara Barksdale and Kami Flavin for reading, proofing, and commenting on the drafts; your words that did not kill me made me stronger. Thanks to Kevin Vain and Rachel Knox and Renee Walker for your publishing kung fu, and to Julie B. Cosgrove for your experienced, professional insights. And thanks to my good friend Greg Aronowitz for your amazing artwork (truly one of the most talented and prolific guys I know). Also thanks to David Godfrey at the Sea Turtle Conservancy, for being willing to have some fun and helping our real turtle friends. And certainly thanks to my business partner David Valentine and our whole agency staff, including Autumn, Derek, Rae, Rachel, Aly, Alex, Alex B, & Trudy, who supported me through this entire process. I also want to thank all my friends who were so patient with me while I toiled away when I could have been out rocking with you! Now it's done. Let's party, Framily!

INTRODUCTION

I truly appreciate you taking the time to read this book. I would not necessarily swear everything you are about to read is the gospel truth, but it is the best recollection I have. Everything was a long time ago with decades of memories and lots of partying since then. Lots.

Let me set the record straight from the top, my real last name is Troum, so if you see my name in the turtle movie credits, it's always Kenn Troum. After living a little while in Hollywood, I realized that nobody can say or spell Troum correctly, so I dropped it and started using my middle name, Kenn Scott. It's easy to say, easy to spell, voila! Now, that's how everybody knows me. Anyway...

This book answers a lot of behind-the-scenes questions I get from all over the world, and shares private stories of how I found myself playing a lead character in one of the most popular film franchises of all time.

I used a lot of my friends real names (because I think and hope they'd be cool with it) and I changed some names (either because I didn't want to exploit anyone, I thought it sounded cool, or I forgot to correct it during editing [sorry]). To everybody else, I named you because people can just look you up on the internet.

I've had lots of adventures since these movies, but these were the beginning of a lifelong association with a character that would forever influence my life. There are many friends and fans that have continued to make me feel special because of that association. I truly hope that any interactions we've had, whether at comic-cons, or just in life, have allowed me to make you feel just as special, as well.

With Love,
Cowabunga!

Kenn

TEENAGE NINJA TO MUTANT TURTLE
Becoming the Reel Raphael

WTF!?

It was the middle of the night and I was under the streets of New York in a dark, dank subway station, sweating like crazy in a green, foam rubber suit. I shuffled along the darkened subway tracks, away from the safety of the lighted station platform behind me. With each step into the murky tunnel, my rubber feet slapped against the dirty wooden ties of the tracks. It became more difficult to see, not just because of the dwindling light, but the tiny eye holes in the foam rubber head limited my vision like crazy.

New York subway tunnels are pitch black worlds of trash, smells, rats, and gross stuff you can only imagine. In my mind, I was sure there were crazy cannibals in the shadows ready to take unwilling prey like me back to their mole-man leader. I was also concerned about accidentally touching the subway's infamous electric "third rail," and getting fried to death.

But, despite some concerns...none of that mattered. I would have done anything.

I was living a dream and this was my big chance. Whether it was crawling through a pitch-black subway tunnel or a murky sewer, I would've done anything to be right where I was.

We were shooting an early scene for the first *Teenage Mutant Ninja Turtles* movie in which the character of April O'Neil goes to the subway and faces the evil gang of ninjas known as the *Foot Clan* for the very first time. She is ultimately saved by the turtle Raphael, who takes her back to the turtles' secret lair, and from there her legendary relationship with the four reptilian heroes begins.

That night, I was lucky enough to be playing Raphael.

The production company had rented out a real subway station, not open to the public due to construction. That way we could shoot throughout the night and not be disturbed by commuters or trains.

To start the scene, the director, an Englishman named Steve Barron, wanted Raphael to emerge from the dark shadows of the subway tunnel, so they placed the camera on the station platform and sent me walking into the darkness. When the director shouted "Action," I was supposed to "ninja walk" my way out of the tunnel towards the light.

Seemed easy enough.

Once I got about 50 yards up the tracks, I faced back towards the lights and crew. The only sound I could hear was my own breathing echoing off the inside of the turtle head. I also think I heard some rats scurrying around, but it could have been my mind playing tricks on me. It was very quiet, very dark and, except for the underlying fear of cannibal mole men, it was kind of peaceful.

As I stood in the middle of the tracks, listening intently and waiting for the director to give me my cue, I kept thinking about how great everything was at that moment. I don't mean how cool it was being in a dank subway tunnel, that sucked. I mean, how cool it was to be in the costume of Raphael the Ninja Turtle, on a film set, living out my dream of being an action hero in the movies.

Ever since I was 13 years old, I wanted to be like all the karate masters, secret agents, and super soldiers I had seen in the movies. I loved Arnold Schwarzenegger, Jean Claude Van Damme, Bruce Lee, Chuck Norris, and anybody else who fought bad guys in action-packed style on the silver screen. Since I was young, it had been my singular goal to be a movie action hero like them, and I had worked hard for it. Now, after dedicating my life to pursuing that goal, I was playing one of the title characters in a Hollywood martial arts film. Granted, I was stuffed inside a big green turtle suit, but it was the greatest thing that had happened to me, and a dream come true. I took a deep breath and thought, "Man, how cool is this?"

Then I heard a low rumble.

I had spent a lot of time in New York, so I knew it was the sound of a garbage truck or cars on the road above the station. Then it got louder, like maybe there was some construction going on up there.

A moment later, a slight wind blew through the tiny holes in the mask. Dust got in and made my eyes water. I thought, "Feels like somebody opened a door somewhere." I blinked several times to clear my eyes, but the wind became more intense.

Then, through strained, watery eyes, I saw it. A light illuminated the tunnel walls several hundred yards away, and it got brighter.

"Holy shit," I thought, "There's a train coming!"

My next thought was, "This can't really be happening." I mean, this was a professional film crew, they must have checked every-thing out and knew that this subway station was closed...right? They wouldn't put me out here if they weren't sure about that... right? These thoughts of professional responsibility brought me a brief second of calm, kind of like the feeling of being on a ride at an amusement park; no matter how scary it is, you know that it's ultimately engineered to be safe, so there's no way anything should go wrong. But, the thing was, this was no amusement park ride. This was the dirty-ass, rat-infested maw of the New York City subway system and crazy shit happens in New York all the time. There are signs that tell you not to stand on the freaking subway track. You're just not supposed to do it.

The light got brighter and the rumble got louder.

My mind raced back and forth, switching between disbelief and absolute fear. I saw the distinct shape of the train's round headlamp come around the curve and I heard the clang of wheels bouncing against the tracks. That's when I realized this was most definitely real. My heart rate shot through the roof! I was about to pay the ultimate price because somebody else had made a scheduling error.

I was frozen. I couldn't see around me because of the mask and I didn't want to end up fried on the stupid third rail. I was literally caught on train tracks with an engine barreling down on me, like a scene out of a movie. The bright light raced closer, blinding me, the rumbling became a ROAR, and the wind was blowing dirt like a sandstorm through the eyes of the mask.

"Shit," I thought, "This is how it ends?" My eyes watered from the dust, but it could just as easily have been tears of fear.

"How!?" I screamed. "How did this happen? How did I get here?"

IN THE BEGINNING...

My grandparents & great grandparents came to America from Eastern Europe for economic reasons and to escape the anti-Semitic persecution that was growing in their homelands. They immigrated to New York by boat, worked in the garment and upholstery industries, got married, and had kids. Two of those kids were Diane Kay Kreiss and Martin Alan Troum, my mother and father. My parents were both born in New York in the 1940s, and both graduated from New Rochelle High School in Westchester County, just outside of New York City. A little while after they met, they eloped.

In 1964, just about nine months after my parents got married, my brother Stephen was born. My mom was only 19 and my dad was just 23, so you can imagine it was a lot to handle for them. They were just a couple of kids in New York with a new baby, trying to figure out how to get by. My father went to school at night, graduated from New York University and started working for a large chemical company while my mother was taking care of the baby. They lived with my dad's parents for a while, but because of my dad's job, they were able to get a tiny apartment of their own. That's when I was born, Kenneth Scott Troum, on May 3, 1967. That year, America was involved in the Vietnam War, Muhammad Ali was stripped of his heavyweight boxing title for not going to war, and the Beatles released *Sgt. Pepper's Lonely Hearts Club Band*. 1967 was also known as the "Summer of Love." 1967 is just a date on my driver's license, and I don't remember any of those things, but I like to think all that cool stuff was going on at the time.

When I joined the family, it was just me and my brother Stephen. He was three years older than me and already a heroin addict. I'm kidding. My brother doesn't have a drug problem. He was actually a very good student and a well-behaved child. He is now a respected hand surgeon who occasionally has a fruit-flavored alcoholic drink.

My brother and I were typical examples of older and younger siblings. Since he was the first child, my parents were concerned with every movement he made, trying to make sure he didn't drown in a toilet or choke on crayons. He was shy, quiet, and reserved. By the time I was born, my folks realized none of those terrible things actually happened to him, so they were a little more relaxed with me. I had a lot more leeway to be adventurous growing up and I took advantage of it. I was active, excitable, and dangerous.

I had a sense of adventure right from the start, often getting into trouble for wandering off in our New York neighborhood, sometimes even getting hurt because I wasn't afraid to try stupid things. At only four years old, it wasn't uncommon for me to end up with a cast on my arm or leg from a mishap at the playground, or even jumping off the top of our bunk beds with a Superman cape pinned to my neck. I ended up at the doctor's office so often that, at one point, the authorities intervened and questioned my parents, suspecting them of child abuse. Fortunately, they realized very quickly that it wasn't that at all; it was me not being afraid of action and adventure, or bad decisions (I'm still not).

When I was five, I was just becoming cognizant of the New York world around me but my father's company transferred us 500 miles south to Greensboro, North Carolina; a very different environment from New York. North Carolina is a land of lush green trees, churches, and NASCAR. It's also a land with wide open spaces and plenty of opportunities to exercise an adventurous spirit.

ACTION HERO FROM THE START

Ever since I was very young, I was drawn to people, both real and fictional, who performed heroic or adventurous activities. This included everybody from real-life soldiers, police officers, and firemen, to fictional characters like James Bond and Robin Hood, and even flesh and blood daredevils like motorcycle rider Evel Kneivel. I was fascinated by these folks because of their physical prowess and by the way they took on impossible odds. They were also usually champions of righteousness, at least the ones from books, movies, and TV. I was intrigued, impressionable, and would do whatever I could to try and imitate these people and their action hero ways.

My friends and I used to play "war" in the woods by our house. I'd wear my dad's old army gear, including his web belt and canteen, and carry a toy gun. We would head out into the woods and run missions. Sometimes we'd divide up into teams, crawl through the leaves and climb trees to get advantageous spots from which we could point our guns at each other and shout, "Pow! I got you."

My action hero interests also included books and movies about medieval heroes like King Arthur and his Knights of the Round Table, or Ivanhoe. There was something about those guys fighting for "right" and achieving victory because of the honesty in their hearts that spoke to me. I used to dress up in armor made of football pads and tin foil and fight my dad with wooden swords

TEENAGE NINJA TO MUTANT TURTLE

and trash can shields. One time I fought my brother Steve and took a bloody chunk out of his forehead with a piece of pipe. He still has the scar.

My brother and I both loved comic book superheroes. We used to save our allowance and go to a big flea market in Greensboro. 1970s swap meets like that one were the precursors to today's comic-cons. There were just a couple of dealers selling comics amongst all the other tables of jewelry, housewares, and assorted junk, but the diehard super hero fans were there every time. Steve and I would spend hours sorting through boxes of comics. *Captain America* was my favorite. He was like a modern-day knight, fighting for truth and justice. I also loved a relatively unknown series at the time titled, *The Man Called Nova*, about a kid who gets hit by an alien ray and turns into an intergalactic cop.

There were also superheroes I worshipped on TV, like on reruns of the old *Superman* show, *Batman*, and *Wild, Wild West*. And I loved pro-wrestling. I mean LOVED IT! My brother Steve and I would watch wrestling every Saturday on TV all day. Our mom hated that.

Greensboro was a major hub of the National Wrestling Alliance (NWA) and we saw championship bouts with Ric Flair and Ricky Steamboat, and watched guys like Jake 'The Snake' Roberts, Jimmy Snuka, and The Iron Sheik in action. Steve and I actually started our own "pro" wrestling league called the *Universal Wrestling Alliance*. We were the only two in it, but it didn't matter. Each of us played multiple roles, including wrestlers, managers, announcers, and referees. We had homemade championship belts and a microphone to interview each other. We acted out complete matches in the living room, choreographed on the spot. Just like the real thing, we learned how to throw each other to the floor or drop kick one another and not really get hurt. My brother, had the coolest wrestling name, "Steve Star." He was our first UWA heavyweight champion.

I don't know why all that action-hero stuff appealed to me as deeply as it did. I realize that a lot of young boys like action and adventure. But for me, it was something deeper, something elemental in my DNA that drew me to both the action aspect, and also the heroic causes that the good guys fought for. I fantasized about facing off with bad guys and kicking their ass on the battle-field or in the ring. All the movies, books, and comics allowed me to escape into the world of the action heroes. All the pretending, the war games, and wrestling was a chance to live out the heroic fantasies. In these worlds of imagination, I was the hero. I always had the skills and abilities to come out on top.

I was to soon find out, that's not always the case.

ATTACK OF THE JERK

It was 1979 and I was in the 7th grade in Greensboro, NC. I was barely five feet tall, playing soccer, being a pretty good student, stealing Penthouse Magazines from a box in our attic, and getting ready for my Bar Mitzvah.

One day, during math class, I was walking down the hall on an errand for my teacher when I sensed something move quickly out of the shadows. I turned and saw Chase Woolen, a kid who had recently moved to our school and was a little rough around the edges. He was darting towards me with a friend right behind him.

Chase wasn't very tall, but he was solid and wiry, with long stringy hair. He wore black t-shirts and smoked cigarettes. We weren't friends, but we weren't enemies either. I didn't even really know him. That's why I'm not sure why he chose to do what he did next.

I think I just happened to be a little guy in the wrong place at the wrong time. Also, I'm sure he had a desire to look cool in front of his friend, or to make up for a tiny penis, but for whatever reason, Chase grabbed me in a headlock and squeezed as hard as he could. Then, with a move straight out of professional wrestling, he did what's called a "bulldog." A bulldog is when you grab a guy in a headlock, throw your feet in the air, and slam your victim to the floor, driving him into the ground with the full weight of your body. You also wrench the guy's neck up at the same time. It's a pretty devastating move when done for real, and this guy did it just right. He slammed me into the tile floor with full force, BAM, and wrenched back on my head and neck at the exact same moment. There wasn't anything fake about it.

I felt an electric surge shoot through my neck and shoulder as I landed on the floor.

He immediately sprung to his feet, pointed at me and shouted, "That's what you get!" and took off laughing and running down the hall with his friend.

The muscles in my neck immediately stiffened up, like somebody was squeezing them in a vise. Tears filled my eyes. I looked around to see if anyone had witnessed what just happened, but there was no one there. I was alone.

It's not the worst thing that's ever happened to someone, but it was sudden and painful, and an attack that left me feeling hurt and helpless on the floor. There was nothing heroic about that moment for me at all.

I got up and made my way back to class, massaging my neck, trying to hold back tears. I explained to my teacher what happened and she attempted to calm me down, saying she would take care of it. I went back to my seat, doing my best to hide my eyes from my classmates.

Luckily, that was my last class of the day and I soon got on the bus and rode home in silence with my head down, my neck throbbing from the pain. I was feeling hurt, weak, and angry. When I got home I didn't say anything to my parents, I just sat in my room and stewed. It took a while for me to calm down.

I was feeling sorry for myself and was mad as hell at that jerk, Chase Woolen. I was angry and wanted the world to be different. I knew I didn't want to ever feel like that again.

That's when I looked in the mirror and made a decision that would change the rest of my life.

I decided to take karate.

VISIT YOUR LOCAL PUBLIC LIBRARY

One of the kids in my school, Bobby Henrik, was taking karate a couple of times a week at the local community center. A few months before I got jumped by Chase Woolen, Bobby had gotten in a scuffle in the same school hallway with another kid. The kid pushed Bobby and swung a looping fist at his head, but Bobby leaned back to avoid the blow and kicked the kid right in the side of the head. Now, truth be told, Bobby didn't knock the kid out or anything cool like that, he actually stumbled back from being off balance, but the kid ran away, and Bobby looked super cool for having done that to him.

I wished I could have kicked Chase Woolen like that.

There was no internet back then, so I went to the public library and got some books on karate. I didn't know anything about traditions, history, philosophy or anything like that, but the books had pictures of stances, punches and blocks that I could imitate. I took off my shoes and started practicing in the backyard, setting these bibles of knowledge open on top of a trash can.

I learned how to do some stances and a few basic strikes, but I was quickly limited by my ability to figure out what I was looking at in the pictures. It was hard to understand the full movements from still images, like trying to learn how to swim from a book. What I really wanted to do was to join Bobby's class at the community center. It was only $15 a month for two hours every Thursday night, and two hours every Saturday morning. That's eight classes a month for $15, or $1.88 per class, a pretty good deal. I asked my dad if he would pay for it.

He listened to my request and suggested it might be just another pastime I would undertake and quit, like building model rockets or model trains. But, because he saw me working hard in the backyard with the books, he decided to make a deal with me: he would pay the $15 every month, but if I quit, I would have to pay him back for each month he had paid.

I didn't even think and blurted out, "Yes, okay!" I was 12, I had no real understanding of money or its value. I wanted to take karate and he was offering me a chance to do it. I would have agreed to any deal.

That weekend he took me to my first karate class.

THE JOURNEY OF 1,000 STEPS

The community center karate class was taught by Lawrence C. McSwain, known to his friends as "Mac." Mac was an assistant district attorney when I joined the class at 12 years old and would go on to retire decades later as a well-respected District Court Judge. As a college student, Mac was a member of the original A&T University Karate Club in Greensboro, NC, along with Space Shuttle Challenger astronaut Ron McNair. The club was known for being a gritty and accomplished group of martial artists that did very well in competitions against much more experienced athletes. Mac was put on this earth to help guide others, whether in the robes of a judge or wearing a black belt in front of a karate class. Mac is also an interesting guy because he's a huge fan of the old West and the history of African-American cowboys. Now that he's a little older, he likes to wear cowboy hats and bolo ties and take his wife Vivian on vacations to see significant western historical spots. I'm sure she loves it.

After my dad signed me up, one of Mac's senior students spent time teaching me the basic moves so I could fall in line with the whole group. I felt good because I had a head start on some of the techniques because of the books. Still, it was hard to do some of them in combination and, at times, I felt totally uncoordinated. The senior student explained that this feeling was part of the learning process and eventually my brain would adjust and adapt to the movements. We spent two hours moving back and forth across a full-length basketball court doing stances, punches, and blocks. It was exhausting...but it was also super cool. I was immediately hooked and started going twice a week.

The training was very traditional and intense. The style, called *Goju-Ryu*, originated in Okinawa and became well-known in the movie *The Karate Kid*. We did crazy amounts of push-ups on our fists, calisthenics, stance training, "thousand-punch" and "thousand-kick" drills, and we learned forms (or *katas*) and fought. Every once in a while, we'd get to work on some unique stuff, like practicing with nunchakus or bo staffs.

I took to it all like a fish to water. I was excited about going to classes and I was pretty good at it. Physically, I had been playing soccer and was somewhat athletic, so I was strong for my size and developed flexibility pretty easily. I readily adapted to the mechanics of the movements. Mentally, one of the things that helped me most was the same thing that allowed me to have fun playing soldiers or knights when I was younger; my imagination. Using imagination as I practiced karate techniques, I was able to visualize my opponents in front of me. When you do that, it gives your techniques great focus and crispness. There is an old martial arts adage that says, "Practice your form 1,000 times and you will begin to see your opponents; practice your form 10,000 times and other people will begin to see your opponents." I wanted everyone around me to be able to see my opponents, so I practiced like crazy.

I really loved practicing with the nunchakus. Swinging those things around was super fun and good for developing forearm strength and coordination. It's also good for knocking the shit out of your elbows, your groin, and your head if you're not careful. I quickly got tired of denting my skull, so I went to the closet and got a skateboard helmet and started practicing while wearing that. That helmet helped me escape a lot of concussions.

I competed in tournaments up and down the East Coast and did pretty well, winning trophies in both forms and fighting. At the big tournaments, I got to see some famous karate stars perform, people that I had only read about in magazines, like Cynthia Rothrock, Billy Blanks, and li'l Ernie Reyes, Jr. Little did I know that someday, I would be on the silver screen with all of them.

I loved the physicality of martial arts training: the punching, kicking, stretching, etc. It was like super hero soldier training and good for working out natural energy. I also loved the philosophical aspect of martial arts. Being exposed to Eastern thought and trying to live by the code of Bushido, or "the way of the warrior," introduced me to concepts and practices that would follow me throughout my life.

After several years of training, when I was 17, Mac came to class and asked me to stand at attention in front of the whole group. I jumped up and snapped into position, bending my knees slightly, my fists poised in front of my waist, ready to spring into action. Mac began talking about my journey as a martial artist from young boy to young man. He talked about the challenges I faced and the steps I had taken to grow. And he talked...and he talked...and he talked. For 45 minutes he talked while I stood perfectly still with my body in a karate ready stance. I was sweating, my legs were shaking, and I wanted so bad to scratch the itch that had been creeping up my back for 20 minutes. It was agony. Finally, Mac reached into a bag and pulled out a black belt and handed it to me. I was thrilled. For almost six years I had worked diligently, practiced hard, succeeded in competition, and taken on the responsibilities of teaching others. Martial arts had become my way of life, and now I had achieved a coveted black belt.

And I didn't owe my dad any money for lessons anymore.

MARTIAL HEROES

One martial arts related practice that became a big part of my existence early in my training was watching martial arts movies. You just can't be a teenage boy and a martial artist and not be interested in martial arts movies. I was a huge fan. It didn't matter if it was Bruce Lee, Jackie Chan, Chuck Norris, Sho Kosugi, Joe Lewis or even James Ryan (anybody? anybody?), I loved them all.

When I was growing up, before cable TV and the internet, you had to go to the theater to see these movies. My dad used to take me and we'd sit in the darkened theaters and watch those guys kick ass. They were everything I wanted to be, good guys fighting for good causes, saving kidnapped girls, bringing killers to justice, and stopping street gangs in their tracks with amazing kicks and flips. I so wanted to be one of them. And it didn't seem unreasonable to think that I could, because you didn't just have to be Asian to do it. Chuck Norris and Jim Kelly are two examples. All you had to do was fight for a good cause and be a kick ass martial artist... maybe even if you were Jewish.

My martial arts action hero fantasies were also fueled by comic book heroes *Iron Fist* and *Richard Dragon: Kung-fu Fighter,* and by a series of books I call, "ninja porn." I don't mean porn like in sex, but there was a series of books called *Ninja Master,* by a writer named Wade Barker, that described violent ninja action and adventure. In the series, the hero, Brett Wallace, is a Caucasian American trained in the Japanese art of ninjutsu. Like the television series *The A-Team*, the hero traveled around the country using his ninja skills to fight against sex slavers, mobsters, and terrorists. In the books, with titles like *Only the Good Die*, *Mountain of Fear*, and *The Skin Swindle*, the author supplies accurate but gory martial arts details like this...

> *Brett's arm came down in the classic shuto-strike karate chop, breaking the man's nose, a spray of red erupting from the pulpy mess. With a quick pivot, he smashed his elbow in the man's face, driving the broken nose bone into his frontal lobe. The thug dropped to the ground, a gurgle and bubble of blood escaping from his mouth.*

I mean that is some serious stuff. Here's one of my favorite classic lines from the book *Million Dollar Massacre* by Wade Barker,

> *The hitman's guts started pouring out from the hole between his legs.*

I mean, c'mon, how cool is that?

So, between the comic books, movies, and ninja porn, I had all this action hero stuff running through my head. At this same time, as a growing boy, I was pondering what I wanted to be when I grew up. Part of me wanted to join the army and be a special forces soldier or be a cop. I also thought I would make a good spy for the CIA.

I realized as I thought about doing all those things, that I really wanted to do them all, but IN THE MOVIES. Not only were the guys in movies doing all the cool action hero stuff, but from one movie to the next, they were doing all the different jobs, whether fighter pilot, detective, or vigilante. They got to do it all, plus they made lots of money, lived in nice houses, and achieved worldwide fame. That sounded great!

I decided I wanted to be an action hero in the movies, too.

Being a movie action hero would fulfil my inherent need to fight for just causes as a kick-ass action dude, but it would also fill a growing desire for the same recognition and validation I gave to my movie star idols. Plus, I had visions of owning helicopters, riding in limousines, and living in a mansion, based on the block-buster paychecks I would earn. Besides, I wasn't going to be just a martial arts movie guy, I was going to become a true action hero that moved beyond kung-fu movies. I could fight aliens in space, mercenaries in the jungle, or spies in the cities. Sylvester Stallone, Arnold Schwarzenegger, and Bruce Willis did it on the grandest scale. But, there were other achievable levels of stardom that made the journey seem even more doable for a short, Jewish kid from North Carolina. For instance, Jean-Claude Van Damme worked his way up through the minor leagues of low-budget karate movies to become a major box office attraction. Steven Seagal was a martial arts instructor who got his big break from one of his students.

I had a pretty high opinion of myself; I thought I was a good martial artist, I perceived myself to be much better looking than I was, and I had total faith that I had the natural acting talent to be as good as the guys I saw on screen. There was just enough for me to sink my teeth into to make me think I could do it. So, from that point forward, I set my mind to making myself a cinematic action hero! And nothing was going to stop me.

ACTION HERO IN TRAINING

The first thing I did was sign up for drama classes in school. I auditioned for and became part of a school theater group that performed plays for the public throughout the year. I had just enough energy and untrained ability to do an okay job and land some lead roles. I even won "Best Actor" and "Best Actor" honorable mentions in competitions that pitted various state high school drama programs against each other.

I also stepped up my martial arts movie-ready skills by competing in karate tournaments in a division they called "self-defense." In this division, you enacted a little self-defense play, like a scene from a movie. For instance, a girl might pretend she was walking down the street and her fellow students would jump out, pretend to be bad guys and attack her. She would launch into a choreographed fight, defeating each one with various techniques. Sometimes it was serious, sometimes it was funny, and sometimes it was amazingly action-packed and exciting with loud music playing behind it. I loved this stuff and immediately got some of my fellow students to do it with me. We got pretty good at it, winning several competitions along the way.

One of the guys in my group, Tony Johnson, actually had a little bit of experience as a professional stuntman. I was fascinated and hounded him with questions. He was a handful of years older than me and had worked in New York doubling a guy on a soap opera and also for a while on a movie called *Sgt. Kabukiman NYPD,* a low-budget, action, comic-book film made by Lloyd Kaufman of Troma Films, the company responsible for *The Toxic Avenger* and *Surf Nazis Must Die.*

I was enthralled by Tony. I thought him having worked on a movie was one of the coolest things ever. He humored my questions with answers, but Tony didn't really know how much the fire burned inside me to even get a chance to do what he had done. I was impressed by and extremely jealous of Tony's experiences at the same time.

I decided to experiment with some video equipment and see if I could shoot some movie-like scenes myself; hopefully stuff I could use to send to real producers or stunt coordinators and see if I could get hired like Tony had done.

I had recently been watching Cannon Films' *Enter the Ninja* and *Return of the Ninja*, in which the star Sho Kosugi performed amazing feats like catching a flying arrow or jumping completely over somebody's head. I wanted to figure out how they made that happen, so I got one of my karate class buddies, we dressed up in some ninja uniforms and video-taped ourselves trying to recreate these moments. We figured out how to use camera angles, learned how to edit in the camera as we shot, and we put together some cool moves. It actually looked like my friend shot at me and I caught his arrow and then jumped over his head with a flying side kick. But, it also looked totally cheap and cheesy. We could never show it to anybody seriously, but we learned a lot. I had such a good time that I decided to try and make a full-length movie.

MINI MOVIE MOGULS

VHS tape video cameras were fairly new technology at the time and made it so anybody could record anything. My friend had one, so we were going to use it to make a full-length, action-packed cop movie.

We came up with an idea about two detectives who are great partners, but one of them gets involved with a drug kingpin and turns on his friend. We called it *Life in the Fast Lane* and figured we would use the song with the same name by *The Eagles* as our theme. We didn't write a script, but we did write down ideas for scenes we thought we could shoot. The opening was awesome. It featured an undercover cop in the middle of a warehouse of armed thugs, buying a briefcase full of drugs. He's wearing a wire and the moment he says a code word, other cops come storming in to arrest everybody and one of the bad guys gets shot. It was totally cool and definitely a rip-off of everything we'd ever seen in real movies.

Another friend's dad actually owned a cardboard box-making factory. He said we could use his factory and as many boxes as we needed to fill up the scenery. I got a couple of guys from my theater class to play the speaking roles and a bunch of our friends who owned guns to play the thugs.

Everybody showed up on the day with the requested costumes and guns. The guys playing cops came in suits, and the thugs came in black t-shirts, camouflage, and sunglasses. And everybody brought lots of guns.

The warehouse was filled with empty boxes and we had chairs and a table for the drug deal to take place. I hung a cheap microphone from a broomstick so we could hold it over the actors' heads like a boom mic. We had just a few lines written out on some loose notebook paper.

We filmed all the clichés, including briefcases of money and drugs, cutting open a bag and tasting the white powder with a finger, etc. When the cops came rushing in, our bad guy, played by our friend Mark, was supposed to shout, "No way man," then pull out a gun and get shot by the hero. The shot is supposed to send Mark flying backwards through the air and crashing through the table with the drugs on it behind him.

For the scene, we filled Mark's hand with ketchup. The plan was that when I said "Action," he was supposed to slap his hand across his stomach to spread the ketchup and leap backwards through the air, crashing through the table.

We took away the real folding card table and replaced it with a rickety stunt table we made out of particle board and duct tape. Mark took his position with the ketchup in his hand. I shouted, "Action," and like a good soldier, Mark slapped his belly with the condiment and leapt backwards, about four feet up into the air. He then crashed through the table perfectly. Unfortunately, the spindly table collapsed under him with ZERO resistance. Basically, Mark fell four feet, straight down on his back, on a concrete floor. He let out a crazy grunt, "Aaargh!"

"CUT!" I shouted.

Mark lay on his back and moaned, "Mmmmmnnnnnnnnhhhhh." He rocked back and forth on the floor. We rushed over to see if he was okay. It took a few moments for him to get his breath and his head to stop spinning, then we helped him to his feet.

I stood in front of him, looking into his eyes, making sure he was okay. In my medical opinion, he seemed fine.

He coughed and whispered, "How did it look?"

I shook my head, "Well, to be honest, you jumped so high you went out of frame."

His eyes fell to the floor.

I gritted my teeth and asked, "Do you think you can do it one more time?"

And he did. Mark was awesome that day and we got the shot. We filmed everything we set out to get.

We went home excited and watched the tape.

And it sucked.

You could barely hear anybody's lines, the acting was stiff, the action was slow and clumsy, the camera angles were uninspired, and everything was totally unbelievable. Terrible writing, directing, and acting. I was heartbroken. In the long run, it turned out to be a great lesson, because I learned what you should NOT do when making a movie, but at the time it was a heavy blow.

If I had been less dedicated to my goals, I may have quit at that point. But instead, I saw the positives. I learned from our efforts, figured out what could be done differently and knew that we could do better on the next shoot. So, we scheduled one for the following weekend.

Our friend with the video camera was unavailable, but my dad was able to borrow a video camera from his job and let us use it. It was an expensive camera, so he was showing a lot of trust in me.

The scene we wanted to film featured one of the cops meeting an informant outside of a local hot dog stand. We used to eat lunch at this hot dog stand during the school year, so they were willing to give us permission to use their patio for our project. We got our actors, coordinated wardrobe, and mapped out the dialogue. I plugged my homemade boom mic into the camera and handed the broomstick to my brother, Steve. I said, "Just hold that over their heads as close as you can, but high enough so it's out of the shot."

"No problem," he replied.

Everybody got in position and I stood behind the camera. I turned to my actors, "You guys ready? Okay everybody...and... ACTION!"

As the first actor stepped into frame, my brother stepped forward to get closer with the mic. Unfortunately, the mic cable was super short and he pulled the camera forward, the tripod toppling over like a felled tree. The whole contraption landed face down on the lens, on a cement sidewalk, CRUNCH!

"Ahhhhhhhhhhh!!" I yelled and quickly scooped it up like my own baby. I looked at the lens and there was a thin white crack running right along the center. I got scared and angry all at the same time. I looked at my brother and screamed, "What the hell?!" It wasn't really Steve's fault but I needed a target for my anger. I had to control myself from jumping all over him. Of course, that was the end of our filming for the day and we hadn't even got one shot done. We packed up the gear and headed home, my heart and head pounding with anxiety.

I hid in my room for a while, but I eventually found my dad and reluctantly told him what happened. Luckily, there were a lot less fireworks than I thought there would be. He was disappointed, but he simply said, "Get it fixed. Or you have to buy a new camera."

Holy crap, that technology was $2,000 back then. I didn't have that kind of money. I only had a shitty minimum wage job scooping ice cream at a Baskin Robbins, and the chances of me having saved any of that money were slim to none.

I opened the yellow pages, found a VCR and video camera repair shop and took it there, hoping I might just be responsible for replacing the lens or something. When I got to the shop, the guy quietly held the camera up and stared into the lens. My heart was pounding. He reached over to his workbench, grabbed a cloth and some furniture polish and proceeded to wipe the lens. "Yeah, it's fine, you just had a little scratch on there, but this took it off. No charge." I stared in disbelief.

"Holy shit," I thought, "are you kidding me? We can start working on our movie again!"

I thanked him profusely, took the camera back to my dad, and told him the good news. He was happy. Then he took the camera back to work and I never saw it again.

That was pretty much the end of my filmmaking days until I got to college.

REDNECK HOLLYWOOD

Even though my friends and I weren't very good at making movies, there were a few people in North Carolina that were producing real movies themselves.

A guy named Phil Smoot lived in my town and made a couple of low-budget exploitation films called *Alien Outlaw* and *The Dark Power*. You could find them in your local mom and pop video stores in those days. In case you don't know, "exploitation film" is the term used to describe any movie, usually low-budget, that exploits single elements like horror, sex, or martial arts to appeal to a certain guaranteed audience. In exploitation films, it doesn't really matter if there are big time actors in the film, only that the fans of the genre get to see the thing they like, whether it's blood, backfists, or boobs. When I was in high school, I didn't know what an "exploitation film" was, nor did I know the real difference between low-budget and big-budget movies; all I knew was that a movie was a movie, and in my mind, they were all equal. That's why this local producer really intrigued me.

I saw an article about Phil Smoot in the *Greensboro Daily News* and discovered that my friend Matt's parents knew him. Being enamored by the wisdom I imagined Mr. Smoot held, I thought if I could talk to him, just like *Obi Wan Kenobi*, he would give me a secret, some advice, or a job, that would help make my movie dreams come true. Matt's folks gave me his phone number and I immediately called.

When I got him on the phone, Phil was very gracious with his time and told me the trials and tribulations he went through to make his movies. He discussed how difficult it was to put all the pieces together, raise the money, and how important it was to find actors with at least a little bit of recognition to help sell his films. For his movies, he had hired an old Western actor named Lash LaRue who was famous for using a bullwhip in the 1940s and '50s. I had never heard of Lash Larue myself, but I found out later that he taught Harrison Ford how to use the bullwhip for his role as *Indiana Jones*.

Phil let me know that because of the expense and incredible amount of work it took, he probably wasn't going to make another movie for a long time, so he didn't have a job for me. But, he did offer me some positive words on moving forward. One big thing he recommended was to get some headshots to share with any other producers I might meet. Having a headshot to send was the only way to be considered for a movie by a director or producer.

About this same time, during my senior year in high school, a friend of mine from karate tournaments had been hired to play a ninja in a low-budget movie shot just a few hours away in Shelby, North Carolina. There was a guy there named Earl Owensby who made independent movies. Earl was a wealthy guy who owned his own movie production facility, as well as a single movie theater in the nearby town of Shelby. He would make movies starring himself, usually some kind of action exploitation film, then he would show the movies in his own theater in town. This qualified him to claim that his films were "theatrically released" in America and he could sell them for more money overseas.

Earl was friends with Elvis Presley and even had the gates of his own small movie studio emblazoned with the letters "E.O." just like the famed "E.P." on the gates of Graceland. Earl had a picture of himself in his studio lobby in which he's dressed in a white, bedazzled jumpsuit, just like Elvis. He would eventually receive a lot of press years later when he bought an abandoned nuclear energy reactor in South Carolina and rented it to James Cameron to fill with water and shoot *The Abyss*.

My karate friend lived near Earl's movie studio and had been hired to dress in a cool red ninja outfit and do stunt fighting for a film called *Unmasking the Idol*. He got to break through fake walls and do a flying sidekick into a fountain. How cool is that? I wanted to do that stuff, too, so I took Phil Smoot's advice and got some headshots taken. They were awful, but they were me. I even dressed up in a ninja outfit and got my dad to take some pictures of me posing with my nunchakus. We did it on a nearby creek because that looked the most like Japan to me. Once the photos were developed, I got in my car and drove to Earl's studios about two and a half hours away. I knew that if I could get in the door and meet Earl, he would hire me to be a ninja, probably also want to make me a star.

When I got to the studio, I walked into the small reception office. It seemed more like a dentist's office than a magnificent portal to movie fantasyland. There was a receptionist tucked behind the window. I introduced myself and she could not have cared less that I was there. I asked to speak to Mr. Owensby and told her I was an actor and martial artist. Again, she could not have cared less. She told me Mr. Owensby wasn't available and asked if I wanted to leave my headshot. Ah-ha! She fell right into my trap; not only did I have a headshot, I had the photographs in my ninja outfit, and even had a letter I had written introducing myself.

Things were working out perfectly.

I thought there was no way Earl Owensby could look at all that stuff, read my letter, and not see the vast potential I had waiting to be unleashed. Although I was somewhat disappointed I had driven all that way and not met him, at least I was there in person handing her my stuff.

I left the office, content that I had done everything I could for my career that day. I stopped at the nearest McDonalds and ate a fish sandwich on the way home, celebrating my effort and anticipating my first breakthrough role in an Earl Owensby film. That anticipation was to last a very long time.

Forever really.

Days, weeks, and months went by, and I never heard from Earl. I called every few weeks and left messages for him with his receptionist, but I never heard back from anyone. However, I didn't let it get me down and just kept pushing forward. I knew I was putting positive energy out there. If nothing else, completing tasks like that delivery and actually making follow up calls made me feel good about my efforts and gave me motivation to do more. I was feeling the satisfaction of being on my journey and knew I would eventually find success somewhere. Every task was a positive use of my energy towards my intended goal. They may not have always been the best strategic moves, but in my brute-like fashion for pushing forward no matter what, doing something towards my goal felt like I was doing something good.

COLLEGE? I DON'T NEED NO STINKING COLLEGE

As high school came to a close and my film star dreams remained unfulfilled, I knew I was still destined for Hollywood, but my parents said I had to get a college degree...just in case acting didn't work out. Oh, what little faith they had in me. But, they were my parents and I was used to doing what they told me, so I created a plan to blast through college as quickly as possible and continue on my path to action hero-dom.

I did very little research and didn't make very wise decisions on where to go to school. I should have gone to UCLA or NYU or some other school with a great film or acting program, but I was naive, so I applied to University of California San Diego and Stanford, just because they were in California. I had reasoned that because they were in California, they must be close to the movie business. In reality, they were nowhere near it. I also applied to the University of North Carolina because it was close to home, and a lot of my friends were going there.

I received favorable acceptance letters across the board, but when it came time to decide where to go, I chickened out and went to nearby UNC. To be honest, I had fears of going off on my own so far from home, and I also thought I was doing my parents a favor because my in-state tuition was going to be remarkably cheaper than what they had paid to send my brother to Emory University a few years before.

31

I arrived at the University of North Carolina–Chapel Hill in the fall of 1985 and the timing sucked for two reasons. First, I was 18 years old that year and they had just changed the drinking age to 21. This law forced college campuses to forbid open alcohol consumption in and around dorms. The second thing that sucked about going off to college in 1985 was that AIDS had entered the national scene and sex became a dangerous and taboo pursuit. Everybody was afraid of getting laid and dying. I was definitely no Casanova, but this kind of cultural threat shut even more doors on my budding manhood. Despite all these obstacles to social development, I was still determined to pursue action hero-dom, so I signed up to get a degree in *Radio, Television and Motion Pictures* and I joined a theater group.

What I really majored in, however, was partying.

Growing up, I was a serious martial artist and didn't believe that I wanted to pollute my body with alcohol. But, one night in high school I drank two fruity wine coolers and had a great time. By the time I got to college, I was drinking beer and cheap white wine every weekend with my friends. Once I got to college, I formed a tight bond with my college suitemates, all ROTC Marines who worked out hard and drank even harder. For us, college became all about drinking, seeing bands, and finding parties to crash. I also smoked pot for the first time in college. It didn't have any effect the first time, but the second time I thought my face was melting off.

Outside of partying, I did like making videos for film and TV class. It was my first chance to get back into production since the hot dog stand incident. An old high school classmate named Steve Marca also went to UNC and took the same production classes as I did. Steve was smart and funny. He had a sarcastic sense of humor and we had a lot of fun together and began to share our dreams of working in the movie business. We agreed to move to Hollywood together after graduation and follow our dreams. He wanted to be a director and I was going to be the next action hero.

CALIFORNIA DREAMIN'

I knew if I was actually going to be an action hero, I had to eventually move to Hollywood, so I figured I needed to go out there and investigate the territory. After my sophomore year in school, during summer break, I went and spent the summer in San Diego living with my Uncle David, my mom's brother. My plan was to hang out for the summer, visit nearby Los Angeles a few times and get the lay of the land.

I got a job as a day camp counselor at the local Jewish Community Center working with 3rd graders and spent my days at the pool, playing soccer, leading song sessions on guitar, and at night fooling around with some of the female counselors. I also spent a lot of weekends with some co-workers, driving south across the border to Tijuana, Mexico. The drinking age there was only 18 and you could have a great time without much money. You just had to make sure you could get back home.

That summer, with $1,000 I borrowed from my uncle, I bought a little MGB convertible and tied some bull horns I got in Tijuana to the front bumper. Then, one day, I took time off from camp and drove up to L.A. to investigate the Hollywood scene.

For my trip to L.A., I grabbed some water to fill my leaky radiator along the way and headed up the 5 Freeway to Tinseltown. After a two-hour drive, and several stops to cool down the car, I eventually got to Santa Monica, right on the beach in Los Angeles. It was full of beautiful people, fancy cars, and expensive homes...

33

and also some crazy looking people. I didn't know anything about getting around L.A. except for what I read on a map (there was no Google at this point), so I was a little intimidated venturing into the spider web of jam-packed freeways and roads that made up the city. I did, however, come up with another brilliant plan to break into the movie business.

I had read that Steven Seagal, who had recently been in the awesome movie *Above the Law,* owned an Aikido school right in the heart of Hollywood. My goal was to get to his school, introduce myself, and blow him away with my awesome talent, of course getting him to introduce me to important people in Hollywood and make me a star. It was the Earl Owensby plan all over again, but this time I was playing in the major leagues.

I stopped at a payphone and looked up Seagal's school in the yellow pages. It had a Santa Monica Boulevard address. I was already on Santa Monica Blvd., so I figured all I had to do was drive up the road a bit and I would run into it. What I didn't realize at the time was that boulevards in Los Angeles are very, very, very long; all the way from one side of the city to the other. Plus, it was nearly 5 P.M. rush hour (a deadly time of day in L.A.). I turned my little convertible northeast on the road towards the venerated dojo and ventured forth full of optimism. That is, until two hours later, when I was still creeping along one of the busiest roads in the world, sweating my ass off as the sun beat down on me. At that point, I was tired, hot, and hating L.A.

But, then, I saw it; nestled in the shadows of the second story of a small strip mall on the corner of Santa Monica and La Cienega was Steven Seagal's Aikido dojo. It was like seeing a holy temple. I found a place to park, grabbed my ninja photos, patted down my wind-blown hair, and headed up the stairs. I could feel my heart beating with each step closer to the door. I couldn't wait to meet the action hero I had idolized on the screen. As I moved past the tinted windows towards the door, I knew I was taking steps closer to my destiny.

I grabbed the door handle and pulled.

And it was locked.

WTF?! I pulled again, just to make sure. Then I noticed the hours posted on the door. The school was only open for a select few hours a week, and today, on Friday, they were closed all day. My heart sank. How stupid I was. I didn't call to check hours, and I had fantasized that the hottest martial arts star of the moment would be sitting at his desk waiting for potential students to walk into his school to sign up for 30-day free trials or some shit like that. I was heartbroken.

I thought about staying the night, but I had no place to stay in L.A., didn't know where to go, and really didn't have any money. I was just planning on being there for the day, and now all I had done was sit in traffic. It was awful. But, rather than get totally depressed, I reminded myself that I had actually accomplished something because I had put positive energy into the pursuit of my dreams. I was following the Law of Attraction and putting positive vibes out there. Granted, the trip was a complete waste of time, but I had shown the universe that I was intent on my goal, and this gave me a sense of satisfaction. Again, it was just like the Earl Owensby trip; nothing had really paid off, but I felt good because I was putting effort into the ether.

I had such a miserable trip that first time, I never went back to L.A. that summer. I was having so much fun working at the camp and partying with my friends that I just stayed in San Diego until it was time to go back to school.

Then the Law of Attraction really kicked in.

THE LAW OF ATTRACTION

The Law of Attraction basically says that whatever you put out into the world is what you will get back. For instance, at the most basic level, if you think positive thoughts and take positive actions, positive things will happen for you. Or if you think negative thoughts, negative things will happen. The Law of Attraction attributes a lot of power to the mind and our connection to the vibrations and frequencies of the universe around us. By focusing our intent on something, we harmonize with those universal vibrations and attract the elements and opportunities that vibrate similarly. A few years ago, The Law of Attraction was repackaged in a book as *The Secret* by some enterprising folks and became a best-seller. Truthfully, the concept has been discussed for centuries. For example, Buddha said: "What you have become is what you thought."

In the Bible, Proverbs 23:7 says: "For as he thinketh in his heart, so is he."

The Bhagavad Gita, an ancient Hindu text, says: "You are what you believe in."

Regardless of the source material or differing religions, scholarly thinkers and philosophers throughout time have all homed in on the concept that "you reap what you sow."

I was living that formula and the mixture was paying off.

I had returned from San Diego and gone back to school for my junior year. I had been doing everything my little brain could think of to pursue my goals. I was getting a film degree, acting at school, practicing movie-style martial arts, making videos, reaching out to moviemakers and stars, and constantly dreaming about being an action star. I was putting my vibration out into the universe in volume.

And my vibration was answered.

Now, I'm not going to claim that I'm responsible for major economic development in the state of North Carolina, but while I was putting all these incredible vibrations into the universe, it just so happens that they built a real-life, full-size, genuine movie studio right in North Carolina, at the beach, just a few hours from my house.

The studio was built by Dino De Laurentiis, a well-known Italian movie producer who produced his first movie in 1940 and would eventually go on to produce hundreds of films, including *Death Wish* with Charles Bronson, *Serpico* with Al Pacino, *Conan the Barbarian* with Arnold Schwarzenegger, and the cult-classic *Flash Gordon* starring Sam Jones.

De Laurentiis had originally come to North Carolina to produce *Firestarter* with Drew Barrymore in 1984. The producer loved working in North Carolina and the experience was an economic boon for the state, so the governor provided incredible tax incentives for De Laurentiis to build a whole brick and mortar studio in Wilmington, right by the beach. At that studio, they shot *Blue Velvet, Manhunter, Maximum Overdrive* with Emilio Estevez, and *Raw Deal* with Arnold Schwarzenegger; a movie in which Arnold, as the town sheriff standing in the kitchen with his inebriated wife, utters one of my favorite movie lines ever, "You shouldn't drink and bake."

When I learned that there was a movie studio being built in North Carolina, I felt that heaven had opened its floodgates to me. I made it my mission to get into that place, no matter what it took.

As soon as the school year ended, I loaded up my car and drove down to Wilmington and found a cheap apartment to sublet.

I was ready. I had my dreams, my ambition, an apartment just a few miles from the studio, and enough drive and energy to overcome anything. There was only one problem.

I had gotten fat.

CHUBBY KENNY

Even though I was taking the necessary steps to pursue my dream, I had been partying too much in school, had stopped working out regularly, and was eating a lot of fast food and pizza. Lots of pizza. Just a couple of years before, I was fighting in karate tournaments at 140 pounds and looking lean and mean. Now, at just five foot seven inches tall, I was bloated to almost 170 pounds and looked like Elvis right before he died. It was terrible and I knew I had to do something if I was to get back on track and have any chance at being the next Jean Claude Van Damme.

My days of wrestling taught me that to lose weight, you eat as little as possible and exercise as much as possible. So, I took two major steps: first, I started constantly exercising. Every morning, noon, and night, I started doing all kinds of made-up aerobic movements. I had seen Jazzercise classes in the same building as my karate class, and I knew martial arts and boxing training techniques, so I started putting it all together in various routines of jumping jacks, high kicks, squats, running in place, push-ups, sit ups, etc. I even started putting on the radio and just dancing around the apartment like I was in the movie *Flashdance*. I swam laps in my apartment's pool, as well as the ocean, and I would go running around the block, a lot. I did this stuff in spurts all day long, every day, trying to constantly burn calories.

39

The second thing I did was severely limit my diet, although not in a very healthy way. Once a day, I would go to Taco Bell and get a single small bean burrito with guacamole. Then I would go to the nearby Swensen's Ice Cream Parlor and get a small chocolate shake. I figured that both those things were at least giving me a small dose of protein and fat to carry me through the day. That's all I ate, every day for several weeks. About 500 calories a day of fat, sugar, and sodium...and no fiber. The plan was to eat like that for as long as possible and lose weight. It wasn't easy, and definitely not healthy, but I didn't know any better. Surprisingly, I kept it up and, slowly but surely, it actually started to work, and I started shedding weight. I had created a terrible fitness program...but it was working.

EXTRA! EXTRA!

N
o matter what kind of shape I was in, I couldn't afford to be lazy, so I got the address of the movie studio and drove by it to scout out the territory. It was located just off one of the main roads.

My heart was pumping as I got closer, not sure what to expect. Then I saw a bunch of fence that you couldn't see through, almost like the walls around a prison. It was kind of anti-climactic, just a bunch of high solid walls. But then, as I drove past the entrance, which was little more than a guard shack at the time, I saw something totally cool. A giant *King Kong* head was sitting on top of the guard shack. I mean, this thing was huge, at least seven or eight feet tall. De Laurentiis had recently produced a film called *King Kong Lives* and somebody thought it would be cool to put the head of the giant gorilla on top of the guard shack. It was beaten up by the rain and wind, but it was frikkin' awesome! It gave me a thrill because it was a little bit of movie magic right by the side of the road. Unfortunately, right under King Kong's head was a security guard with a badge who was keeping all the lookie-loos out of the magic factory, including me.

They didn't just let anybody in the studio. It wasn't the kind of place that offers tours or anything like that. Short of being an official crew or cast member on a film, the only way you might be able to get inside the fence was if you were an "extra" or "background performer" on one of their films. So, I decided that's what I would do.

I learned there were two extras casting agencies in the city, Fincannon and Associates and Action Casting. My understanding was that the two companies mostly kept their stable of performers exclusive. In other words, if you worked for one, you probably wouldn't work for the other, at least not on anything super cool. This was important because, unlike Hollywood, there weren't a lot of productions happening at any one time in Wilmington, so landing a film was a big deal for these small agencies. As a performer, if you signed up with the wrong agency, you might not work for a while if they didn't get the contract for the next film that came to town.

I did some research and discovered that the Fincannon Agency was doing a lot of work recently, so I made an appointment, brought my headshot package to one of the owners, Mark Fincannon, and told him my goals. I told him I wanted to be an actor and this was a chance for me to be on sets, experience what it's like, and try to pursue my dreams. What he heard was "blah blah blah." The guy didn't care about my dreams. I'm sure he had heard it a hundred times before. He handed me forms to fill out, took a polaroid photo, and proceeded to explain the rules to me.

"When you're on set, you listen to the AD (Assistant Director). They will tell you where your holding area is, the bathroom, food, etc. Don't talk to the actors, don't ask for autographs, don't talk to the director or anybody else except other extras. You understand?"

I nodded, "So, is there a lot of work at the studio?" I asked.

He shook his head, "No, it's mostly on location. We have people we've been working with for a while that work inside the studio."

My heart sank, but I was bolstered by the fact that maybe he'd like me enough to move me up the ladder. I tried to make more small talk, but he was too busy to bother with me and sent me on my way.

I felt pretty optimistic about signing up. Now, I just had to wait for him to call. In the meantime, I would try to figure out other ways to get into that studio.

LOCATION HUNTING

In the 1980s, the North Carolina Film Commission advertised the studio and resources in Wilmington as "Hollywood East" and tried to lure various productions to come to town. Living in the city, you could always tell when a movie was on location in the city filming because you'd see lots of white trucks parked together and one would have a giant portable generator hitched behind it for powering all the lights and equipment. If you saw one of those trucks and the "gennie" behind it, you could be certain there was a film being shot somewhere within 50-75 yards because that's how far the cables would stretch. They might be filming in residential houses, restaurants in the middle of town, or a bar down by the waterfront. Sometimes you'd see off-duty cops sitting on their motorcycles on the street corners making sure traffic was controlled around the set. You could also see crew members hustling back and forth along the sidewalks, and huge, bright lights pointing in the windows of a nearby building, showing you exactly where the shots were taking place. Once you learn to recognize them, these working encampments stand out like a sore thumb.

I trolled through the city every day looking for movie crews. When I found one, I would park a block away, walk over, and stand as close as possible to just watch and listen. It was a chance to see and hear real movie production crews in action. I could see all the people, vehicles, and logistics in action, and it all fascinated me; the massive lights and gear, the prop and costume trucks, even

44

the grips moving stuff back and forth. A "grip" is a person on a movie or television set that helps move all the equipment around the set; literally they get a "grip" on things like the camera dolly, cables, C-stands, and other equipment and move it around.

On these excursions, I learned to spot the Assistant Directors or AD's. AD's are responsible for making sure everybody is doing what the director wants. They're like drill sergeants on a movie set.

The 1st AD works closely with the director, relaying all the director's commands to the various crew members and keeping the movie production rolling along throughout the day.

The 2nd AD works for the 1st AD and takes care of a lot of paperwork. The 2nd AD is also usually responsible for controlling all the extras when they are on set. They are like the head babysitter. The 2nd AD chooses which background performers to take in front of the camera and then places them around the set according to the director's orders. Amongst veteran extras, it was not uncommon to bring offerings to 2nd AD's including beer, wine, or anything else they thought might help them get selected for prime, on-camera assignments. If it was a male AD, the cute girls always got the best spots. If it was a female AD, they were often pretty butch and the cute girls still got the best spots.

The more I was able to watch these people and the movie sets in action, the more I was able to pick up on some of the language and customs of the industry. For instance, here's some things you might hear on a movie set:

"**Rolling!**" = Everybody be quiet and stop moving, the camera is recording.

"**Cut! Back to one.**" = Stop the action, everybody go back to the beginning of the shot and get ready to do it again.

"**C-47**" = A clothespin. Usually used for holding colored filters over lights.

"**10-100**" = In the bathroom.

"**Martini Shot**" = This is the last shot of the day.

Whether it was learning the language of the set, identifying the different department workers, or even catching a glimpse of a famous actor, by sitting on the outskirts of a set, it was amazing how much you could see and hear if you were quiet and paid attention. I knew that the more I listened and learned, the better prepared I would be when my opportunity knocked.

DRACULA'S WIDOW

Within a few days of signing up with the Fincannon Agency, I got my first call. I was hired to work as an extra on *Dracula's Widow*, a low-budget horror movie starring European softcore star Sylvia Krystel. Ms. Krystel was a Dutch model and actress who, several years before, had starred in a series of provocative films as the title character Emmanuelle.

Dracula's Widow, directed by Francis Ford Coppola's nephew, Christopher Coppola, was about Dracula's ex-wife (Krystel) coming to Hollywood and biting the manager of a wax museum (Lenny Von Dohlen). In my particular scene, I was to be one of several patrons in the background of a bar called "The Blue Angel."

When I arrived, I checked in with the 2nd AD and with all the other extras, was sent to the wardrobe truck to get costumed up. I was so excited. In order to match the gothic-noir tone of the picture, the director had us all dressed in early 1940s fashion. For the guys, this meant wool suits...in North Carolina...in the summer. That can get pretty hot. Fortunately, the shoot was at night and the ocean air kept the city somewhat cool. This was my first time working on a real live movie set, getting ready to be in front of a camera. Putting on my wardrobe felt like I was donning armor preparing to go into battle...and it was hot in that suit.

After getting dressed, we were shown back to our holding area and then sat around and waited...and waited...and waited. For hours, crew members were going in and out of the bar, equipment was being moved, AD's were shouting "Rolling!" and "Cut!" But, the extras weren't any part of it. I was to discover then, and over the rest of my career, that if you're a performer on a movie set, mostly what you do is wait; waiting for lights to be set up, waiting for the cameras to be moved, waiting for make-up to be applied, waiting for the sun to get to just the right spot to shoot. "Hurry up and wait!" people always joke. Then, after all the waiting, when they're ready for you, they roll the camera, shoot something really quickly, and then start the process all over again, waiting for this and waiting for that. For an outside observer, it can be tremendously tedious. For me, it was awesome. Even sitting at the empty catering tables, talking to other extras, watching the people work, I was drinking it all in.

Then the AD showed up and shouted, "Okay folks, we need some people inside."

This was it! We put our things away and formed a line, filing to the set. I became more giddy with each step. We made our way past the generator and followed the thick cables running along the ground. They disappeared under the black curtains that surrounded the bar, protecting it from unwanted streetlights. My heart was beating fast as the AD parted those curtains and we stepped inside.

My eyes adjusted to the smoky darkness and I saw that we were in a plain bar with some tables and chairs scattered about the floor. Nothing exceptional, but dark and mystical enough to me. As I scanned the room, I noticed inky black curtains that had been hung in the recesses to cover light stands and equipment, I saw crew members milling about in the shadows, climbing ladders, and hoisting lights. Then I saw the camera; a great big 35mm film camera mounted on a dolly, the big camera stand with wheels that can be pushed around on the floor or put on tracks to get a smoother shot. Even though I was several yards away from the camera, I just stared at it. That amazing machine from the days of Thomas Edison is what made all this possible. It was the key to my dreams and also super cool to look at with all the buttons and lenses and dials.

I was shaken out of my stupor by the AD, 'Hey you! Come sit over here."

He led me to a seat at the bar...close to the camera. Hot dog! The camera was just to my right, shooting my profile. I realized that I wasn't going to be just some extra lost in the deep background, my face would be featured prominently in the shot. Awesome!

The AD then got one of the cute female extras and said, "Here, you come sit with him," and he sat her to my left. More awesome!

"You guys act like you're talking to each other," he said, and then he proceeded to rotate our bar stools. He turned her so that she was looking directly at me, into the camera beside me, and then he reached down and rotated my barstool counterclockwise, to face her...making it so my back was turned directly to the camera, the camera only seeing the back of my head.

What?!

Wait, I thought, I'm supposed to have my face seen on the screen.

"Ok," said the AD, "you guys stay like this, act like you're talking but don't make a sound. When we're not rolling, keep it quiet so everybody can work."

I was frustrated, but immediately came up with a plan to still get my face on camera.

About then, the actors were brought in, including the star Sylvia Krystel. I didn't know a lot about her and her best days of sensual European nudity were behind her at that point, but I did know that she had been in movies, and that's all that mattered, she was a star in my eyes.

Sylvia and another actor set up at the bar right by us. They discussed the scene for a bit with Chris Coppola and then, when everybody was ready, the director shouted "Action!"

It was time for my big screen debut.

Just like the AD said, the girl and I acted as if we were talking, but we didn't make a sound. They tell you that if you're not good at pretending to speak silently, you should just mouth the words "peas and carrots" over and over. She was doing that. Then I pretended that she said something funny and I laughed big (silent, but big). When I did, I craned my neck all the way around until the camera could see the side of my face.

They finished the scene, the director called "Cut," and the AD called "Back to one." Then we did it again. And I did the exact same thing again. And then they did it again, and so did I. This went on for several takes and nobody told me to stop. After that it was pretty much them moving the camera to different angles and filming different parts of the same scene over and over. I just kept doing the same thing, thinking I was going to be all over this movie. (When it finally came out on VHS tape, I saw the film and all you see is the back of my head. They cut out my laugh...probably because they looked at it in the editing room and said, "That guy looks like an idiot when he's laughing.")

While we shot inside the bar, they were using a smoke machine to create visible atmosphere. I would come to find out over the years that they used this same type of smoke machine on almost every movie I worked on. The purpose of a smoke machine is to fill the set with a light fog that disperses harsh lights and gives the set a dusky vibe. This is especially true of mystery movies, horror movies, thrillers, and any historical, dusty setting. There are various kinds of substances used to produce this smoke, including wax and mineral oil. None of them are good for you and they can really dry out your eyes. After working on the set for a few hours, it feels good to go back outside and breathe clean air. Fortunately, we got a break when the AD called "Lunch, one hour!"

Lunch on a movie set doesn't mean noon. Lunch on a movie set means you're exactly halfway through your 12-hour workday. Our workday started at 7 P.M., so lunch would be at 1 A.M. and we could plan on being dismissed at 7 A.M. For some people, this can be screwy, and mess up their whole circadian rhythm, but I love night shoots. I love being up all night doing something I love. I love the idea of being productive and getting things done while everybody else is sleeping. I love driving home at eight in the morning after a hard night of work while everybody else is just driving to work. I love drinking a beer or two at 8:30 in the morning before shutting all the curtains and going to sleep.

Dracula's Widow was my first experience with all those things, and it was incredible, both for how boring it was and how awesome it was at the same time. I lived off the energy of that first night on the set for the next couple of days.

Within a week, I got another call, this time to work on a film called *Collision Course* starring Pat Morita and Jay Leno. That's right, "Mr. Miyagi" and *The Tonight Show* guy. Many people know that Jay Leno was a comedian, but they don't know he also pursued acting. He actually had a small part in an early film that I loved about the creation of rock-n-roll called *American Hot Wax. Collision Course* was an early version of the *Rush Hour* movies starring Jackie Chan and Chris Tucker that were to come years later. Jay played a Detroit cop and Pat Morita played a Japanese cop that was sent to America to solve a crime. Hijinks ensue as the two conflicting personalities learn how to get along and defeat the bad guys. In one scene, inside police headquarters, I was in the background as a drug dealer being hustled through the station by a cop. I made sure to put up a good fight as I went through. One time, the AD told me to "bring it down" because I was pulling too much focus away from the primary actors on camera with all my movement.

In between takes, I actually spent a couple of minutes talking to Jay Leno about *American Hot Wax*. When he learned I saw the movie, he said, "Well, that proves at least two of us saw it."

PIZZA MAN

After *Collision Course*, there was no more work to be had for a while and I quickly realized that you can't depend on the frequency, or pay, of being an extra to support yourself. I had to get a job.

I couldn't get a regular job because I would have to miss work every time an extra gig came up. The way around that was to sign up for a temporary service. With a temp service you could call in and find work on a daily basis. Now mind you, I'm not talking about office temp work in a sweet air-conditioned building with cute co-workers. I didn't have any office skills. I'm talking about physical labor temp work. I'm talking about real grunt work in hot, dusty settings with overweight, sweaty guys for colleagues. Over the next couple of weeks, I worked an assortment of hard labor jobs. I rolled up giant spools of carpet in a warehouse, I sorted wood at a lumber yard, and I hauled 50 pound sacks of flour and sugar at the Krispy Kreme donut factory. It was hot and heavy work, and it sucked.

During the days when I wasn't working these shitty jobs, and there were no movie sets to find, I basically hung out at the beach, visited with new friends I met on the set, or I stayed in my apartment doing exercises, determined to lose the weight I had gained at college. I did not have cable or an antenna for my TV, so it only got one station with a lot of static. The only thing it would pick up was a local station showing episodes of *The Young and The Restless* soap opera. During lunch breaks from work, I got hooked on that damn show.

After a while, the temp jobs were too crazy, sporadic, and just generally sucked, so I got a job delivering pizzas for Dominos. This is when Dominos still had a 30-minute guarantee or your pizza was free, so you basically had to drive like an action hero to get it there on time. I quickly realized that everybody happily opens their door for the pizza guy because, let's face it, who doesn't want all that hot, cheesy goodness.

That gave me an idea.

I put on my pizza delivery uniform, got two empty pizza boxes and drove up to the movie studio guard shack with the giant King Kong head on it. The security guard stepped out with a stern look on his face. I could feel my heart pumping and my hands trembling.

"I've got a delivery for production," I managed to croak out, knowing "production" was the general term used to describe whatever movie crew was on the lot at the time. The guard looked at his clipboard, then back at me. He frowned. I was sweating. He leaned towards me, like he was going to grab me.

"Yeah," he said, laying his hand on my door. He pointed into the studio lot. "Just follow the yellow line around to the back-lot, they're back there." Then he opened the gate and waved me through.

I tried to control my excitement as I drifted past him. I also tried to keep my shaking hands from swerving my vehicle right into his shack.

Once I was past, I couldn't believe it. I had breached the walls...I was inside the movie studio!

I followed the road to the back of the movie studio property and found myself in the parking lot right next to what's called the "backlot." A backlot is where they have fake city streets and buildings that can be dressed up to look like New York, Chicago, or anywhere they want. It's mostly made up of facades, which are just the fronts of buildings supported from behind by beams. When you're standing on backlot streets, whether it's at Disney, Universal, or even the small studios in North Carolina, you can feel like you're in a whole other part of the world. It's real Hollywood magic.

I parked my car, took off my Domino's Pizza shirt and hat, put on my jeans jacket (this was the 1980s), and walked around the corner. And it was like entering a wonderland.

I found myself in the middle of a bustling movie set, with people, equipment, and activity happening all around. They were filming an action scene with a car chase that ends in a gunfight.

And I was in heaven.

Having been around movie sets, I knew there were so many people involved that if you just laid low and stayed out of the way, you could kind of blend in. I backed up against one of the walls, out of the way, and watched for the next 30 minutes as stuntmen screeched their cars to a halt, fired guns, and took squib hits. A squib is a small explosive device that's placed under clothing to simulate a bullet hit. It's triggered by a battery switch and can be covered with a small condom full of fake blood that bursts. Watching them shoot this stuff was one of the coolest things I had ever seen.

While I was watching, I met the lady in charge of casting the extras that were occupying the town. It was Martha, the owner of Action Casting, the company I did not sign up with when I first came to town. I introduced myself. We got to talking and I shared my martial arts background and goal of becoming an action hero. Martha smiled and told me about a "secret project" involving martial arts that was going to be coming to town and asked if I would be interested in auditioning.

"Of course," I said.

She couldn't tell me much more, but she got my name and number and said she would be in touch if it came to fruition. At that moment, the crew broke for lunch and I had to go before anybody became suspicious of the lost pizza guy.

I could hardly contain myself. By making my way past that security guard, not only did I find myself in the middle of a movie set and got to see some really cool stuff, but I had met somebody who could cast me in a martial arts movie! I was continuing to prove to myself that I was on a path to my destiny.

Unfortunately, there wasn't any extra work to be had for the rest of the summer, but I considered it all a success; I had worked on a couple of movie sets, learned a lot about being on a set, and made contact with casting people who were interested in my martial arts abilities...and believe it or not, I lost 30 pounds on my Taco Bell/ice cream diet and exercise plan. I had stuck religiously to my diet and even had visible abs for the first time in my life.

I made it back to school and limped through my senior year. I kept calling Martha to find out if the martial arts movie was coming any time soon, but she just kept telling me they hadn't heard anything yet and to be patient. Then, one day I called and she gave me the worst news I could have heard; the martial arts movie had decided to go film in Canada, where tax incentives would make the film that much more inexpensive to produce. It wasn't going to happen.

I was heartbroken. And I hated Canada.

It was 1989, I was 21 years old, about to graduate college, and I thought it was all going to be so easy to take my next steps to action herodom with an opportunity like that right in my own backyard. Now, it was no longer an option and I had to plan on making my move to Los Angeles and start my career there, from square one. I convinced myself that this had always been my plan to begin with, so I hadn't really missed out on anything. I put my head down and plowed through the school year, just waiting to graduate and get to L.A. I spent the rest of the semester going to the gym and learning about proper nutrition and exercise, building muscle on the body I had whittled down over the summer. I got in great shape, had some great party times, and graduated with a degree in Radio, Television, and Film, in four years, from a prestigious state university...with a grade point average of 2.3.

I'm sure mom and dad were really proud.

My parents had been divorced and each remarried by this time, so my plan was to stay at my mom's house in Greensboro for a bit and then head to Los Angeles, and nothing was going to stop me.

Then I got a phone call.

Martha from Action Casting called and told me that the "secret martial arts movie" had decided not to film in Canada after all and was coming to town very soon to start production. She invited me to come down and audition.

It was called *Teenage Mutant Ninja Turtles*.

TURTLE HISTORY

Kevin Eastman and Peter Laird were friends and comic book artists. One night, during a brainstorming session, Kevin drew a turtle with nunchakus strapped to his forearms and they laughed about the idea. Peter followed up with a more refined drawing of the unique character, and then, for fun, Kevin added more turtles with different weapons, ending with Peter contributing even more details and adding Teenage Mutant to the name Ninja Turtles. As they were thinking and laughing about the various characters that might be in a Ninja Turtle universe, Kevin went to the kitchen, placed a cheese grater over his wrist, and said, "Beware of the Shredder," and the evil villain was born.

With no large companies willing to produce and distribute their title, they took Peter's $1,500 tax refund check, and a small loan from Kevin's uncle, and they produced a little over 3,000 black and white copies of the first issue. They took out an ad in one of the comic book trade publications, sold the issues to some stores, and it quickly sold out. So, they printed it again. And it sold out again. Then they knew they had something.

Mark Freedman, an astute licensing agent, also recognized that the guys had created something unique and convinced them to let him try to expand the turtles into other media and merchandise. He first hooked the guys up with Playmates Toys, who partnered with an animation company called Murakami-Wolf to produce the first turtles cartoon series and accompanying toys in December of 1987.

They were basically making half-hour commercials for the toys, but the series started gaining some traction with young viewers.

At the same time, the comic books also caught the attention of Gary Propper, a road manager for stand-up comics. Propper loved the idea of making a turtle movie and found a movie producer who could help him named Kim Dawson. Together, they convinced Kevin and Peter to let them option the live-action rights. They then hired another comic named Bobby Herbeck to write a script. One famous low-budget movie producer, Roger Corman, wanted to purchase the script and suggested that stand-up comics Gallagher, Sam Kinison, Bobcat Goldthwait, and Billy Crystal, could dress in turtle shells and paint their faces green. Propper and his buddies turned down that idea and eventually made a deal with Golden Harvest, a company out of Hong Kong that produced Bruce Lee's original films. This company was owned and run by legendary Hong Kong film producer Raymond Chow, Bruce Lee's business partner. Because of Chow's martial arts movie making expertise, Golden Harvest was going to make a low-budget movie with Hong Kong stuntmen in cheap rubber suits for about $2 million. Luckily, one of their executives, an American named Tom Gray, had kids who were fans of the Murakami-Wolf animated series and he got the idea to do something bigger and better. Tom found a partner in Bob Shaye, the risk-taking head of New Line Cinema, an independent film distribution company. New Line had massive success with the *Nightmare on Elm Street* series and now they were looking for another franchise that could help them grow even more. The Ninja Turtles seemed like the perfect fit, so Golden Harvest and New Line cobbled together $8M, hired the Jim Henson Company to design cutting edge animatronic suits, and found a fledgling movie studio in North Carolina that could save them a lot of money.

PAT'S FOOT

The producers decided to shoot the movie in North Carolina because it was a "right-to-work" state. That meant, unlike Los Angeles, where movie producers are obligated to contract with labor unions that demand high wages, North Carolina-based films could hire non-union workers at non-union rates. Actors still had to be from the Screen Actors Guild, but everybody else, including most of the crew and the background performers, or extras, could be non-union. This included the Shredder's evil army of ninjas, or "Foot Clan." Action Casting was responsible for finding local North Carolina martial artists to spend nine weeks on set, dressed in ninja costumes, and get beat up by the Ninja Turtles, for $75 a day...before taxes. The title of the job would be "special abilities background performer," or just a fancier way to say "extra."

The day of the audition finally arrived and I left my place in Greensboro early in the morning to drive the four hours down to Wilmington. I had been told to prepare to demonstrate my martial arts. We were going to have an opportunity to present our skills to Pat Johnson, a legend in the martial arts world.

Pat Johnson was the chief instructor at Chuck Norris' original Tang Soo Do school in Sherman Oaks, CA in the 1970s. He learned martial arts while stationed in Korea and was a tough and respected karate tournament competitor in the 1960s. Pat was an on-camera performer in *Enter the Dragon* starring Bruce Lee and taught Ralph Macchio and Pat Morita how to do karate for the hit film *The Karate*

Kid. If you watch the original Karate Kid film, Pat is the mustachioed referee at the end managing the final fight between Billy Zabka and Ralph Macchio. Pat Johnson is martial arts royalty.

I was nervous, but I had been competing for years, had won awards in choreography competitions, was a good wrestler from my days with my brother, and I lived, ate, and breathed martial arts movies, so I felt I was ready.

I drove onto the movie lot, right past the same guard shack I had slipped through the year before. It felt good to be let in legitimately this time. My hands were not shaking on this occasion.

I parked my car in the assigned lot and walked over to the soundstages. Although soundstages are basically nothing but empty warehouses, they are still fascinating structures to me: they have the potential to house any world built inside them. Being around them felt like being around the pyramids or some kind of holy temple, I was that much in wondrous awe.

My good feeling was soon undermined as I turned the corner and saw over 100 other martial artists waiting to get inside and audition. They were in various martial arts uniforms, all stretching and shadowboxing, or just standing around talking to one another. Many were from nearby karate schools I recognized from my days at tournaments, but a small portion had come from surrounding states, some from as far as Chicago and New York.

If there's one thing every good martial artist knows, it's that there is always somebody better than you out there. That's immediately what I started thinking as I looked at all these guys. I thought there was no way I would be able to outperform all of them. There were just too many. It was a distressing thought. But then, I caught my breath and remembered that this was everything I had been training and hoping for over the last several years of my life. This was an opportunity to open a door to the film business as a legitimate onscreen performer and get paid to do karate in a movie. I knew I had what it took, I just needed a chance and this was it. I settled my nerves and focused on what I had to do.

I found Martha and her assistant Libby and we greeted each other warmly. They signed me up on a big yellow legal pad and told me to wait with the others until they called us in.

I wandered through the gathering crowd of martial artists to find a place to warm up. I said a deferential "hello" to some of the older black belts I recognized, but I did not join a social circle or spend my time talking to anyone. I was totally focused. I put on my karate uniform and tied on my black belt.

Soon, the large metal doors on the side of the building were raised, letting sunlight into the dark structure. There was a big, empty concrete floor with a few scattered gym mats spread around, and off to one side were folding tables with folks sitting behind them.

We were all ushered in and there, sitting behind the table, in tiny jogging shorts and a sleeveless muscle shirt, with a fanny pack across his waistline, was the legend himself, Pat Johnson. Pat's moustache was just as impressive and imposing as it was in *The Karate Kid*. It was obvious he had command of the room because everybody's energy was focused on him. Martha and Libby sat to one side with the list of performers and Pat's principal assistant, Barbara Goldstone, sat beside him with a notebook and pen in hand. We were all seated and Pat stood up, clearing his throat and grabbing everyone's attention with his low, resonant voice.

"Welcome, everyone," he said. "My name is Pat Johnson and I am the stunt coordinator and fight choreographer for this film." He explained that each one of us would have a chance to perform one at a time and present our martial arts in some way, either by doing one of our forms, shadow boxing, or in whatever other manner we thought would help show off our best moves. If Pat liked what he saw, he would ask for more, then move on to the next stage, which was having one of his assistants throw kicks and punches at you to see how well you react, as if taking a hit.

In movies, we always think the hero is powerful because of his amazing punches or kicks. But, the truth of the matter is that it's the bad guy that makes the hero look strong by reacting so devastatingly to the hero's techniques. For instance, if a hero throws a punch at a bad guy and the bad guy's head snaps back, the hero will look strong. But, if the hero throws the same punch, and the bad guy's head snaps back, plus he flies backwards and dramatically crashes through a wall, that makes the hero look super powerful. This is a Hollywood insider secret; it's the stunt guys that make the hero look like such a badass, because they know how to react dramatically to fake hits.

Martha and Libby called our names one by one and each guy got up and did his thing. There were mostly karate guys, but some kung-fu practitioners, a handful of other disciplines, and even a world champion kickboxer. Some guys were pretty good, some not so much, but we all clapped politely after each one demonstrated their moves. After waiting for about an hour, they called my name, or at least tried to, it sounded like, "Kenn Troom."

I stood up and made my way to the edge of the mat. I had competed in lots of karate tournaments, so I wasn't nervous performing in front of a crowd, but at that moment I was nervous about performing in front of Pat Johnson. As far as I was concerned, he held my entire fate in his hands. I had the opportunity to make it or break it at that moment. I took my place in the center of the mat and Pat spoke up, "Kenn, what are you going to do for us today?"

I took a deep breath, "I'm going to perform a kata called Seinchin," it was a routine I had successfully performed in many tournaments. I dried my hands on my uniform, brought my feet together, and bowed deeply.

63

In martial arts, you bow for many reasons, including a show of respect. You also bow to take a moment to transition to your warrior mindset, taking a moment to become mindful and calm. Years of repeating this action over and over before katas and sparring matches develops powerful mental conditioning, allowing you to clear your mind and focus on the task at hand as you rise from the bow. I stood up straight with a long exhale of breath. Then I exploded into my kata. I put everything I had into it; ten years of training, dreaming, and hoping. I thrust my arms and legs into crisp punches and kicks, visualizing my opponents and seeing my techniques cracking their jaws and ribs. My stances were deep and I moved with power. My thick karate gi snapped with the techniques. I punctuated my strikes with loud shouts of "Kiai!" My yells echoed off the walls of the soundstage. When I was done, I received enthusiastic applause from the crowd.

The single minute it took to perform that kata was exhausting. It was like doing a full sprint. When it was over, I was winded, my stomach puffing in and out like a bellows. Regardless, I stood up straight at attention. I knew I had to appear calm and ready for more. Pat spoke up, "Very good. I see you brought some weapons."

I responded with gusto, "Yes, sir!"

I ran to the edge of the mat and grabbed my kamas, a pair of bladed sickles with a loop of leather cord on the bottom of each that allows you to swing and spin them around. I was a little nervous because one time at a tournament I was spinning them and one of the cords broke, sending the sickle flipping up into the air. Luckily it landed safely on the empty gym floor several yards away and not in the crowd. I was especially nervous at this moment because I knew that I would definitely not get the job if I lost a sickle and accidentally killed Pat Johnson.

I pushed the fear of manslaughter from my mind and blasted through the form. I whipped the kamas around and bounced them off my neck, arms, and legs. I jumped in the air for a double front kick and then a tornado kick. I committed to every strike, block, kick, chop, and cut like my life depended on it. When it was done, I was totally gassed out.

Pat asked me, "Very good, Kenn. Can you do any other weapons?"

I sucked wind, "I can do…(huff)…the nunchakus…(puff)."

"Well, great, let's see that," said Pat.

I trotted to the back of the mat and grabbed my nunchakus, taking five quick breaths to try and saturate my lungs with oxygen. I came back to the center of the mat and spun the sticks around, bouncing them off my body, switching hands, and even tossing them in the air. I had actually developed my own signature move. I could spin the nunchakus over the back of my hand like a baton, creating an effect that looks super-fast and appears more impressive than it actually is. After a minute or so of spinning them around as best I could, I caught the two ends and bowed. I fought to catch my breath. Pat nodded his head in approval and said "Great. Put those down and let's do some reactions."

One of Pat's other assistants, a kid from a local karate school, stepped onto the mat and squared off with me. Under Pat's direction, he threw punches and kicks at me to test my reactions.

If there is one thing I can do, it's pretending to get hit. Years of mock pro wrestling matches with my brother helped me hone athletic histrionics beyond what a grown man might be expected to possess. Combining that with the experience of several years competing in fight choreography competitions, I had a pretty good ability to appear like I was getting the shit beat out of me. I knew I had this part of the audition down. When the assistant threw the blows, I spun through the air like I got hit with a sledgehammer and kicked by a mule. I sold it like a pro.

"Okay," said Pat, "thank you very much."

And that was it.

I was dismissed.

There was no congratulatory applause, no balloons or confetti, just a quiet dismissal and they were on to the next guy.

As I left, Martha thanked me and said, "We'll let you know."

I made my way back to my car, caught between confusion and hope. I couldn't tell if Pat liked me or if I had nailed the audition or not. I threw my stuff in the trunk of my car and started the four-hour drive back to Greensboro. I kept playing the audition over and over in my mind. Was there anything I could have done better? Did they like me? I was filling myself with anxiety. This Ninja Turtle audition felt to me like one of those moments where my whole life could change, but it could also leave me feeling hopeless if things didn't work out.

When I got back to my mom's house. I walked inside and saw the answering machine blinking. I listened to the message. It was Martha.

"Hi Kenn," she said, "I just want to let you know, Pat Johnson liked what you did and wants you to come be one of the Foot Soldiers for the film. You need to be at the studio at 8 A.M. next Monday to start rehearsals. Congratulations! Please call if you have any questions."

I practically jumped out of my shoes.

My first job out of college was being a ninja!

GET TO WORK

Because I had been hired as a "local," I had to find my own place to live in Wilmington. My friend Steve Marca was still planning to move to L.A. with me, but because I was now going to be delayed making the movie, he decided to move to Wilmington with me and see if he could get a job working in production. We'd be roommates, gain some valuable experience in the industry, and save up money before we headed west. We got an apartment in the same complex I had lived in the year before.

There were no jobs available on the TMNT film, so Steve immediately checked what other movie projects were registered with the film commission office. He also started driving around the city looking for productions taking place. After some detective work, he found a production assistant job with a movie that was just starting a month-long pre-production process. The movie was called *Tune In Tomorrow*, starring Keanu Reeves, fresh off his success from *Bill & Ted's Excellent Adventure*. Steve started a full summer of working as a production assistant with 14-16 hour days...for very little money. But, at least he was working on a film and would gain valuable experience. I was also about to start gaining valuable experience...also for very little money. But, I didn't care, I was just happy to have a job on a movie, and we were both ready to go!

Driving to my first day on the set of TMNT was cool. It was now the third time I had driven through the studio gate, and this time, for the first time, I was there as an official, paid performer.

I parked, walked to the soundstage, and saw Pat Johnson standing at the doorway, focused on his wrist watch. "Good morning, Kenn."

"Good morning, sir," I said as I passed by.

Other guys followed me in and Pat greeted them the same way, "Good morning, gentlemen."

Then a minute or two later, another guy walked through the door. Pat stopped him and said, loud enough for us all to hear, "Young man, I want you to know that call time was 8:00 A.M., it is now 8:01. Do not ever be late again. If you are, you will not have another opportunity to be late. Do you understand me?"

The guy nodded, and we all got the message. Pat explained that we were professional performers on a movie, where time is money, and we should never, ever be late...ever!

Before I go on, let me tell you a little more about Pat Johnson that I learned as time went on. Pat is one of the toughest men I have ever met. He radiated self-confidence. The license plate on his Corvette read, "I NV NONE." I would not want to get in a fight with Pat Johnson. I feel that even if you were beating his ass, Pat would refuse to believe that a "pussy" like you could defeat him, and he would keep getting up until you couldn't fight him anymore, and then he'd beat you up.

Once we were all inside, I saw which of the guys had been chosen from the audition. There were about 20 of us. I recognized one of the guys as Dale "Sunshine" Frye, the world middleweight kickboxing champion I had seen at the audition. Dale was a local North Carolina boy and one of the funniest, most engaging guys I ever met. He was friendly to everybody and made you immediately feel welcome in his circle. We would spend the next several months becoming friends, but initially I was just excited to be around such a talented and well-known martial arts fighter. Dale had already worked on Cyborg with Jean Claude Van Damme (one of my favorite action heroes of the time) and he would go on to work in several other films later, including Brandon Lee's final film *The Crow.*

Pat's assistant Barbara took attendance, then Pat explained the basic rules. Number one, we were always to be on time, at the risk of our jobs. Other than that, we were to report to that particular soundstage as our "Foot Headquarters" every day; we were to do whatever Pat asked us; we were to bring all questions or issues directly to him; and we were to act in a professional, respectful, and hardworking manner, no matter what. He informed us that we were going to spend the next two weeks, before shooting started, working through choreography required for the action scenes. This time period was Pat's chance to determine what each of us would do throughout the film.

The first step was to get us outfitted, so they marched us to the wardrobe building. We filed past a table, stated our name, and received a plastic bag filled with knee and elbow pads, a black mask, a headband, and forearm guards made out of rubber but painted to look like metal. We also got black pants and shirts, a black, elastic girdle to secure the top and bottom of our outfit together, wristbands, split-toe ninja boots called "tabi," and long pieces of black cloth to wrap and tie around the tops of our boots. I was thrilled because this time I didn't have to sew my own ninja costume together for some backyard photographs. The lady from the wardrobe department explained how we were supposed to put all the pieces on correctly. Once we were all dressed identically, we were a formidable sight; truly an army of badass, black-clad ninjas ready for a fight!

We made our way back to the soundstage or "Foot Headquarters." The stage was outfitted with several gym mats, wrestling mats, and high-jump pads that would allow us to practice falling and hitting the floor. Outside of that, there were just some long folding tables and chairs. Even though the environment was drab, we all knew that we were doing something totally cool and the energy was electric.

We circled around the mats and Pat introduced us to the rest of the stunt team. In addition to his assistant Barbara, there was Pat's main stunt guy, Tom DeWier. Tom had doubled for Ralph Macchio in *Karate Kid III*. He was a professional Hollywood stunt-man who specialized in high falls. Tom would be one of the foot soldiers when needed, would double the Shredder for the high fall at the end of the film, and he would help Pat set up any other complicated stunts.

In addition to Tom, Pat introduced us to a small group of stunt-men from Hong Kong. And when I say small, I don't just mean there were only four of them, I mean they were small. I'm not a big guy and these guys were tiny. They had worked in Jackie Chan movies, barely spoke any English, and were working as stunt doubles for the turtles and the Shredder. They had names caught between Chinese and American interpretations of their Chinese names; they went by Wil (*Michelangelo*) Nam (*Raphael*), Mo (*Leonardo*), and Billy (*Shredder*). There was one more guy named Brandy who was there as a "martial arts consultant," and helped communicate Pat's choreography to the stunt guys in their native language. I was surprised at how good Brandy was, mostly because he was stoned all the time. You could smell marijuana smoke coming off of him. Regardless, I was in awe, replaying every kung-fu movie I had seen over and over in my head and imagining these guys working on them in some capacity. They were the real deal.

In addition to those guys, *Donatello* was being doubled by the amazing Ernie Reyes, Jr. Ernie was about 17 years old and from San Jose, California. He was already famous in the martial arts world for being a child prodigy. Years before, his dad had started a famous demonstration team that performed all over the country at tournaments, special events, and on television. The team featured Li'l Ernie Reyes Jr. as a six-year-old superstar, kind of like a young

Michael Jackson of martial arts. When Li'l Ernie came out and performed, he electrified the crowd with moves and showmanship well beyond his years. Ernie already had some movie and television appearances under his belt including, *Red Sonja* with Arnold Schwarzenegger, *The Last Dragon* starring Taimak, and a starring role in a short-lived television series called *Sidekicks* with Gil Gerard of *Buck Rogers* fame. Ernie was basically a prince in American martial arts royalty. I knew how impressive Ernie was from seeing him over the past ten years, so I was pretty much in awe of him, as well as the whole stunt team. From the Foot soldiers to the stunt turtles, the set was filled with a wide variety of amazing martial artists.

TURTLE TEAMS

There were four guys that played each one of the turtles in the original films. The first guy is the "actor" turtle. This is the guy that wears the main costume and provides all the movement for the body of the turtle. He wears a turtle head that has 27 remote control electric motors, or "servos," mounted inside that control the eyes, mouth, cheeks, etc.

The second guy that plays each turtle is the puppeteer that controls those 27 servos from behind the camera. These guys were from the Jim Henson organization, and had worked on *Sesame Street*, *The Muppet Show*, and the films *Dark Crystal* and *Labyrinth*. Each one of the puppeteers had a large metal travel case filled with a variety of high-tech controls that looked like they could fly a space shuttle. The Henson group called it "puppetechtronics." The controls remotely activated a computer suspended underneath the turtle's shell, and those signals traveled up a series of cables attached to the turtle head to bring the 27 servos to life. In addition to hand controls, each puppeteer wore a headset and microphone. The headset had tiny lasers that pointed to the lips, chin and cheek. When the puppeteer said a turtle's line, like "What's up, dude?," the lasers would pick up the movements, send a signal to the computer, and control the various servos in the turtle's head to say the line.

The third group of guys to play each turtle are the "stunt" turtles. These guys wore turtle suits exactly like the actors, except no computers or electronics inside.

Finally, when the movie is finished being shot and edited, the fourth guy responsible for bringing each turtle to life records the turtle's voice during post-production [*Post-production* is all the editing, special effects, music, sound mixing, etc. that takes place after the actual shooting of the movie is completed].

Besides those four guys making up each turtle, every once in a while, additional doubles were brought in to do special stuff on an as-needed basis. For example, there is a scene where Donatello is skateboarding through the sewer system having some fun. In order to accomplish this, the producers brought in a professional skateboarder named Reggie Barnes and dressed him as Donnie. If you watch that scene, and go through it frame by frame, you can actually see a shot of Donnie's turtle feet on the skateboard, and then Reggie's human hand passes quickly through the frame as he does a 180 on the board. They didn't bother to put turtle hands on Reggie because they didn't think they would see his hands, but it accidentally flashed past the camera. It's so fast, you'd never notice it without stopping right on the frame.

CREATING THE FIGHTS

In order to choreograph the fights, Pat Johnson was given a complete storyboard of the entire film, basically a comic book version of the whole movie script, drawn out, shot by shot, on over 200 pages. A storyboard artist is paid to work with the director and draw a panel for every different shot in the film. It helps the director envision the film and provides a checklist of shots to get in order to make a complete movie. Other department heads use the storyboards to begin visualizing what they will need to make, prepare, or purchase to bring the film to life.

Pat's job was to interpret the action drawn in the storyboards, work with the various stunt turtles and Foot Soldiers, and create fight sequences that would match up with the frames of the storyboard. He started by positioning the stunt turtle performers around the mat, then adding Foot Soldiers, building each fight, piece by piece, adding techniques and moves that would eventually lead to the desired outcome indicated in the drawing.

To start the choreography process, Pat had brought in three or four guys for the Foot Clan a few days before the rest of us showed up and worked through some ideas with them. These guys were his elite team and played very important roles in the initial choreography. Unfortunately, I was not in that elite group and was not being used a lot during the initial few days of choreography. This killed me. Even though I was working as a Foot, my ultimate goal was to get discovered and be an action star, and that wasn't going to happen sitting on the sidelines while other guys got to do all the cool stuff. What also wasn't going to happen sitting on the sidelines was me qualifying for my Screen Actors Guild card, and for every budding actor, getting your SAG card is like getting the holy grail.

THE ELUSIVE SAG CARD

Getting a SAG card for an actor is a special occurrence. It means you have membership in the union of professional movie & TV actors known as the Screen Actors Guild. While union membership doesn't actually get you jobs, it ALLOWS you to be hired for those jobs on union movies and TV shows, which is pretty much all the big ones.

Unfortunately, getting a SAG card is a big "catch-22." You can't get a SAG card unless you perform (i.e. have speaking lines) in a SAG movie or TV show; but you can't perform in a SAG movie or show unless you have a SAG card. WTF?!?

Here's the way around this. If a producer or director sees you in a play and thinks you're fabulous, or meets you in the street and thinks you're beautiful, or is related to you and wants you to be in their movie, they can fill out some special paperwork with SAG and give you the job, and then you get to be in the union. The dream of all movie extras is that the director will see you on set and like you so much that he or she will give you a line of dialogue, on the spot, to say in the film, thus propelling you into the union. This rarely happens. Mostly, you have to become a good enough, or desirable enough talent, and be seen enough at auditions, that a director or producer will be willing to hire you and fill out all that paperwork.

Each time Pat completed the choreography for a piece of action, whoever was playing the Foot Soldiers in rehearsal would be the ones to perform those same roles in front of the camera when it was time to shoot. Pat's assistant Barbara would write down the scene number and the name of each performer that was to do it on camera.

With each successive piece that was being choreographed, I sat on the sidelines watching and listening. Pat kept calling on the same small group of Foot Soldiers for every task, over and over. The rest of us were there just to be background performers if they needed Foot in the background...the deep background. I was in agony. Each time my name wasn't called, it was like my Hollywood dream was slipping away. Didn't they know they had the next Hollywood action hero standing right in their midst? I sure did. I was frustrated and getting more and more despondent.

Then came the skateboard stunt.

THE SKATEBOARD STUNT

There's a scene in the movie where the turtles are fighting Foot Soldiers in the sewer. At one point, Donatello skateboards through the tunnel and uses his bo staff to knock a fleeing Foot Soldier off his feet, sending him high into the air, crashing to his back. For the rehearsal process, Pat had Brandy, the Hong Kong martial arts consultant, acting as Donatello. Brandy held Donnie's bo staff and ran forward as if he were riding on a skateboard. The chosen Foot Soldier was to run in front of Brandy, and when Brandy swung the staff, the Foot had to throw his legs off the ground, pitching himself into the air, and slam down to the ground on his back.

Pat called up one of the elite team and I could only watch as the guy lined up next to Brandy, ready to perform the coolest thing we'd done yet.

Pat yelled, "Action!" and the Foot Soldier and Brandy started running. After about 15 feet, Brandy swung the bo at the guy's feet. Now, instead of hurling himself in the air in stride, the guy literally stopped in his tracks, positioned his feet on the ground, and jumped up in the air, like he was springing off a diving board. He didn't get very high and kind of flopped onto his side.

"No, No," shouted Brandy in clipped English, "No stop like this."

Pat stepped forward, "You've got to do it all in one smooth motion, you can't come to a stop like that. Try it again."

They lined up again, Pat shouted "Action," and at the end of 15 feet, the same thing happened. The guy planted his feet and did an awkward, sideways flop.

"No good. No stop," screamed Brandy.

Pat stepped forward again, "Alright, let's get someone else to give this a try." He turned to all of us waiting patiently. I stood up straight hoping he would pick me. He pointed, "You, Larry, c'mon."

Larry Montgomery was an older guy I knew from karate tournaments. He lined up next to Brandy and took off running. When Brandy swung the bo staff, the exact same thing happened. Larry stopped in his tracks, positioned his feet, and jumped awkwardly through the air, landing on his feet before crumpling to the ground. Nothing about it looked smooth or realistic.

I was amazed these guys were having so much trouble. It seemed so easy. Larry tried it a couple more times, each time Brandy shouting "No. No stop" and Pat trying to offer corrective advice. I could see their frustration growing.

Then I decided to take my fate in my own hands.

I stepped up to the interpreter, a local Chinese kid named Sam whose dad owned a nearby Chinese restaurant.

I said quietly, "Tell them I can do this."

Sam turned to me, "What did you say?"

I spoke a little louder, trying not to be heard by any of the other guys around me, "Please tell them I can do this."

Sam looked at me for a moment and then walked over to Brandy. He spoke in Cantonese, pointing his finger back in my direction.

Brandy looked up and pointed at me. "Okay, you come," he said.

Pat signaled me over, "Come on up, Kenn."

Suddenly, all eyes were upon me. My palms were sweating. I felt pretty sure I could do the stunt, but I was nervous with all the attention. I lined up next to Brandy, my heart pounding.

"Ready," said Pat, "Action!"

I took off running with Brandy chasing me a few feet behind. My adrenaline was pumping. Brandy quickened his steps to close the distance between us and swung the bo at my feet. Out of the corner of my eye I saw the staff flying towards my legs. Just as the bo came near me, I leaned back and flung my legs in front of me, like I was running up an invisible wall, my body completely horizontal. "Oh, shit," I thought, "This is gonna hurt." Then I crashed straight down. I fell like I had practiced so many times in all my wrestling and karate training, with one arm extended to slap the ground, one leg extended, and my body turned slightly to one side. It was a pretty solid thud to the ground. It didn't feel great, but I knew it must have looked good. I looked up to Pat Johnson to see if he approved.

Brandy shouted, "Yes! Yes!" He sprang over to help me up and patted me on the back, giving me the thumbs up sign. "Good, very good," he said and nodded to Pat.

Pat Johnson turned to Barbara, "Very good. Please put Kenn down for this one."

And I was in.

From that point forward, everything was different. Each time they started to put together action sequences, Brandy would confer with Pat and then they would ask me to join them.

I would then follow Pat's commands on the moves he wanted me to perform. Most scenes were just about getting beat up by the turtles, but it didn't matter. I was now part of the elite team and getting used in just about every sequence.

A FELLOW 'CHUCKER, AY?

One of the days when we were working through the choreography, Pat remembered my audition and asked me to do some moves with the nunchakus. He also asked a couple of other Foot Soldiers to do the same. We each had thirty seconds or so to demonstrate our moves.

Pat watched and whispered in his assistant Barbara's ear. She left and returned a few minutes later with David Chan, a producer, originally from Hong Kong, who worked for Golden Harvest. Pat called me and the two other Foot Soldiers out to perform our moves for David one at a time. I spun the 'chucks around as fast as I could, bouncing them off my arms, legs, hips, and shoulders. All the training I had done when I was younger while wearing a skateboard helmet came into play. I did my unique spin move, flipping the nunchaku over the back of my hand like a baton and catching it perfectly. When we had all completed our routines, David Chan pointed at me and said, "Okay. Use him." Then he walked away.

Pat indicated for Barbara to write my name down again. "Okay, Kenn," he said, "you'll do the nunchakus scene."

And just like that, I was assigned my first real featured part. It's the scene in the movie when all the Foot Soldiers crash into April's apartment. Michelangelo looks at one of the Foot Soldiers and says, "Oh, a fellow 'chucker, ay?" and they trade nunchaku moves back and forth. I was going to be that Foot Soldier.

Later, after the movie came out, they made a series of trading cards featuring moments from the movie. Years later I would come to find out there's actually one of me in the Foot uniform spinning those 'chucks!

SHOE FETISH

W e continued rehearsals and, one day, while we were warming up, I felt a strange pressure on my foot. I looked down and there was a long-haired dude, on his knees, with his hands wrapped around one of my sneakers. I heard him say, "Yeah, I'm thinking something like this."

He was talking to a woman standing nearby with a clipboard, I recognized her as part of the wardrobe department that had given us our Foot costumes at the beginning of the production. The guy continued, "I think it should be something athletic, but durable for combat, ya know? I like thése different colors."

I wasn't exactly sure what was happening. I said, "Hello?"

The guy turned up to me, his long hair falling away from his face. I immediately felt like I knew him from somewhere. He said, "Hey man, I like your shoes. I wanna wear something like this." The sound of his voice was familiar and he extended his hand to me, "Hey, I'm Elias." He pronounced it EL'-EE-US, with the emphasis on the first syllable.

I shook his hand, "I'm Kenn. Nice to meet you."

He pointed at the black and red Nikes I was wearing, "I really like those shoes, man."

At that moment, Pat Johnson walked over, "Hi, Elias." Pat turned to me, "Kenn, this is Elias, he's playing Casey Jones, the turtles' friend that helps them kick ass." Then he turned to Elias, "Kenn is one of our action guys."

Elias smiled, "Cool, man. Thanks for letting me look at your shoes. I'll see you around." Then he wandered off talking with the wardrobe lady.

Then it dawned on me. Elias' face and voice were familiar because I had seen him in a movie called *Some Kind of Wonderful,* in which he delivered a brilliant performance as a mischievous, bald-headed punk rocker. I didn't know who he was at that time, but I loved that character.

Elias turned out to be such a good and gracious guy throughout the shoot. As time went on, he became friendly with a small group of stunt guys, including Tom DeWier, one of our fellow foot soldiers on the "elite" team named Paul Beahm, and myself. Every once in a while, we would all go out to dinner. There was something about Elias' take on the world that was different than your average Joe. He wasn't like anybody I had ever met before. He seemed to be a true artist, like a poet. He was meticulous about his diet at the time, trying to stay lean and cut for his role as Casey Jones. I think he was an interesting and great choice to play the role. The director, Steve Barron, made deliberately nuanced choices, casting the movie more like an arthouse film than a kung-fu fantasy with rubber reptiles. Elias was a big part of that.

After meeting Elias, I became more curious about what characters were in the movie and what the story was about. I had never read a Ninja Turtles comic or knew anything about the turtles' world, including characters like Casey Jones or April O'Neil, so I wasn't really sure what was happening in the story. As a lowly Foot performer on the movie, I was not given a script to read. Only important people on a movie crew get scripts, like the actors, director, and all the department heads, so they can understand what equipment they need and what's expected of them and their team throughout the shoot. The scripts are pretty well protected.

One day I had to stop by the office to do some payroll paper-work and I saw a stack of scripts on one of the desks. When I was done with my paperwork, I casually picked up one of the scripts and walked right out the door without missing a step. When I had a chance to go through it, I saw that it had all the storyboards and everything, just like Pat's script. What a score! I took it home and devoured it, learning all about the film and the characters. I went through and took note of all the action scenes we had been choreo-graphing, including the "fellow 'chucker" scene." I felt like I now had a unique insight as to what was going on in the production.

GODS OF CREATION

Being on the Turtle set during these initial days of rehearsal was amazing because of the interesting and noteworthy people that came through. My time with some of them was very brief, but it was always exciting. One of the most thrilling was the day I met Jim Henson, the creator of the Muppets.

We were busy working on choreography, and all of a sudden, one of my fellow Foot Soldiers pointed and whispered, "Hey, look, it's Jim Henson." I looked up and there he was, walking into our soundstage to see the stunt turtles in action. I felt like I was watching a religious figure enter the room. With his six-foot-three frame and familiar flowing hair and beard, he looked like a hippie-ge-nius-emperor. He had come to visit the set in North Carolina to see how his team was doing and he was being escorted around like the royalty he was. Although I did not spend significant time with him, I did say hello, shook his hand and felt a thrill to be in his presence. He sounded so much like Kermit the Frog it was amazing (for the record, Grover and the guy who throws fish are my favorite Muppets).

Jim stayed and watched for a few minutes and then left the stage to move on to the next stop on his tour. I was so giddy I couldn't believe it. After all the childhood years of watching *Sesame Street* and *The Muppet Show*, I couldn't wait to tell my brother I had met him.

Unfortunately, it was only a few months later that Jim Henson became ill and passed away. It was a sad day for the world.

In addition to Jim Henson, two of the most notable people that visited the set while we were preparing to shoot were TMNT creators Kevin Eastman and Peter Laird. They were two regular looking guys who somehow captured lightning in a bottle.

Since I was just one of many "extras" on the set, it wasn't like they were there to spend time meeting me. They were there to see their vision being brought to life in a Hollywood film. They were already successful because of the success of their comic book and the animated series that had recently launched, but I know it must have been a real thrill for them to see their characters and the world they created come to life in live action.

Luckily, I caught them at just the right time. Kevin and Peter had actually brought a stack of Ninja Turtle comic books with them and were giving them away. I made my way over to them, introduced myself, and received one of their comics. They were very gracious and actually autographed it. It's still in my turtle treasure chest today.

Years later, when I was living in Los Angeles, I developed an acquaintanceship with Kevin Eastman. We met repeatedly at some mutual friends' birthday parties, dinners, etc. I was very curious as to what Ninja Turtles had meant to Kevin's life. In very candid conversations, Kevin shared with me that in all the years since Ninja Turtles, he lamented he wasn't able to sell one other significant property to a movie studio or comic book company. He and his partner had struck gold with the turtles and the rest of his professional life was a quest to try and create another hit. He's a very talented, nice guy, but it just goes to show you how hard the entertainment media business is. I mean, he and his partner changed the world and even he was having trouble getting another gig.

I asked Kevin about the impact turtles had on his life, specifically from a financial point of view. After the turtles were a hit, most of us assumed that he and his co-creator Peter Laird were driving around the world in gold-plated, turtle-shaped limousines, right? Well, according to Kevin (and I might get some of the details wrong), he and his partner made a deal with a licensing company that they would get 6% of all licensing deal profits.

Let's break down what that really means…

When you create an intellectual property, like TMNT, you own 100% of the creation. The problem is, you probably don't have the connections or business knowledge to distribute or exploit that property to any great degree. Sure, Kevin and Peter were able to print and sell their own comic books for a while, but the outreach was somewhat limited and there's only so much money in that. The real money is in licensing.

Licensing is when somebody pays you a certain amount of money, or promises you a percentage of profits, to let them put your creation on lunchboxes, t-shirts, or even make television shows and movies about it. With deals like that, your outreach can be millions.

Kevin and Peter made a deal with Mark Freedman and his company Surge Licensing. Mark believed in the turtle property and wanted to rep it around the world. Freedman secured millions in licensing deals for the turtles. The only thing is, according to Kevin, the deal was that he and Peter split 6% or six cents of every dollar of profit. So, imagine that the turtles made $100 million in licensing fees (I'm making this number up), that's a lot of money. At 6%, Kevin and Peter get $6 million of that…but wait, $2 million gets paid to agents and lawyers for putting the deal together and another $2 million or more goes to taxes. That leaves $2 million split between Kevin and Peter, or just a million each. Not bad, but not at all what you might have expected they made. And on top of it, Kevin told me that no matter what he made, he ended up with three ex-wives and a money-losing endeavor when he bought the magazine *Heavy Metal*. So, in the long run, he didn't have a whole lot to show for creating one of the most popular franchises in history, other than a good story. I don't know Peter, having only met him once, but I believe he kept some creative controlling rights to the turtles and may have managed finances a bit more conservatively.

NEW FRIENDS

Each day, when Pat was ready to begin working, he would call us all to attention and run through the various fights we needed to work on that day. The Hong Kong stunt guys and Ernie would practice with turtle heads on so they could get used to the limited vision and breathing challenges. Those things were a real pain in the ass.

The only place the performer could see out of a turtle head were two tiny holes just underneath the turtle's bandana mask, right above the turtle nose. Peripheral vision was non-existent, so doing fight choreography was a tremendous challenge. If you were facing one direction, fighting with an opponent, you could not see the next opponent coming at you from either side. You really had to get the timing down and operate off loud audible counts. The stunt team spent hours going over each sequence to get this.

The guys from Hong Kong were amazing. Outside of filmmaking, simply as a martial artist, this was my first exposure to hard-core kung-fu practitioners from China. Yes, I had seen some great guys at tournaments, but these guys were Hong Kong-homegrown, movie-level martial artists. They were small, skinny, and awesome. Everything they did was circular and fluid with great power.

One day, somebody brought a kicking shield that had a pressure meter built into it. The meter would measure the pounds per square inch you put into your kick. The guys lined up to punch and kick and compare their results. At one point they compared side kicks, a kick Bruce Lee was known for doing with explosive power. A lot of the Foot Clan were kicking the shield and generating between 300 and 900 pounds. Pro boxers can punch with force somewhere between 500 and 1,000 pounds. I'd like to say that I kicked it at 1200 pounds, but the truth is, I don't remember, it probably wasn't that strong. What was more important was that Billy, the guy who doubled the Shredder, stepped back and did a skipping side kick just like Bruce Lee, and kicked that bag at 1700 pounds. Nobody else came even close.

Nam (*Raphael*) and Wil (*Mikey*) barely spoke any English, but Billy (*Shredder*) could speak enough for us all to be able to communicate together. Because I was being used in a lot of the fight choreography, I was spending a lot of time working with these guys and we quickly developed a friendship, trying hard to communicate across the language and cultural barriers. I discovered that during our days off, on Sundays, they just sat around their hotel rooms doing nothing. So, one day, my roommate Steve and I offered to take them to the beach. We all had a great time hanging out. After that day off together, for the rest of the shoot, during off hours, we'd all cram into Steve's little two door Honda and either go eat or visit the mall. One time we even drove them an hour and a half south to hang out in Myrtle Beach, South Carolina, a very well-known tourist destination.

When it was time to eat, these guys didn't venture too much out of their comfort zone. All they ever wanted to do was go to *The Hong Kong House*, a local Chinese restaurant. They would speak to the waiter in Cantonese and order amazing and crazy looking traditional Chinese dishes. They weren't ordering typical things off the American menu like shrimp fried rice or beef and broccoli. Their table was filled with steaming plates of traditional roast chicken, sliced pork, and bowls of rice. Even though I came from a family of New York Jews, who are supposed to know really good Chinese food, I realized at that time that I had no idea what real Chinese food actually was. There's no sugary sauces or platters of egg rolls, or crispy noodles dipped in apricot sauce...it's birds with faces still on them and plates of roasted, odd looking meats.

These guys would have all the dishes placed in the center of the table and then dive in, using chopsticks to shovel food directly into their mouths from the serving plates. There was no spooning portions onto their plates. It was more like a free-for-all to grab whatever you could and get it to your mouth before it was all gone. Watching them plow through the meal, it seemed like they hadn't eaten in days, or thought they wouldn't get another chance. They also didn't care about European-style table manners. If they grabbed a piece of chicken, they would shove it in their mouths and if there was a bone in the meat, they would simply lean over and spit it directly onto the table beside their plate, amassing a little pile of bones next to their setting throughout the meal. And they loved to drink Coke, always Coke.

One day they asked if I would like to eat with them. I tried to explain that I was a vegetarian, but I ate fish, so I could not eat the pork or chicken dishes they ordered all the time. Not to worry, Billy told me. He went into the kitchen. I could hear him speaking in Cantonese to the cook. Soon, two dishes came out and were placed on the table. Being a little-traveled white boy at the time, I had never seen anything like it. I was expecting shrimp in lobster sauce or some other Americanized seafood dish with which I was familiar, but what was placed in front of me was a heaping mound of boiled shrimp, with the heads, antennae, shells, and tail still on, and an entire fried fish, with tail, eyes, and scales. At that moment, I was like "What the hell is this?"

Very quickly, the Hong Kong guys dove into the plates. First, they grabbed the shrimp and broke off the heads, sucking the juice out, then cracking through the shells and chowing down on the meat. They thrust their chopsticks into the fish and pulled tiny slivers of meat out with amazing dexterity. I was so fascinated that I sat and stared, quickly realizing I better get involved if I didn't want to go hungry. I grabbed a shrimp, broke off the head and sucked the juice. I picked at the fish as best I could, trying to avoid eating the ultra-thin bones. It was all so simple, not covered in sauces or sugar or anything we are used to in American fare...and it was delicious. It wasn't long before there was a pile of shrimp shells, heads, and antennae all over the table, and the carcass of a fish picked clean, not to mention the towers of chicken, duck, and beef bones they had amassed next to their plates.

I had stepped outside of my food comfort zone for the first time and was richly rewarded. I felt so blessed to be hanging out with these guys and meeting so many interesting people. I was most definitely on an amazing adventure.

THE PLAYERS

During rehearsals, the director Steve Barron, or producers like David Chan or Tom Gray, would come into our soundstage and see what Pat had going on, approving or altering action for the film as needed. These guys were real movie makers. The executives, David Chan and Tom Gray, were everyday guys in casual business clothes, but the director, Steve Barron, had a little magic about him.

Steve was a very well-known music video director in the 1980s. He made some of the biggest music videos of the early MTV era, including Michael Jackson's sidewalk-lighting *Billie Jean*, the sketched world of A-ha's *Take On Me*, and the computer animated video for Dire Straits' *Money for Nothing*. Steve had worked with Jim Henson's company previously on the television series *The Storyteller*, a bizarre *Twilight Zone* meets *Grimm's Fairy Tales* show. He was hired to direct the film because he proved he had unique vision and worked well with the Henson organization. It was fun to watch him work, and on top of it all, he had a super cool English accent.

In addition to the director and producers, sometimes the guys who were the "actor" turtles would come watch us rehearse, so they could understand what their characters were going to be doing throughout the fights. During the action scenes, the turtles were usually making quick quips, so the actors and puppeteers would step into the scene for a moment or two if there was a line of dialogue that needed to be said in between the punches and kicks.

Like everybody else I saw on this first big job, I was fascinated with the actors...jealous, too. Even though I was excited to be a Foot Soldier and starting on my Hollywood action hero career as a "special abilities extra," the actors were doing what I really wanted to do. They were performing and being the stars of the show. I don't mean being a "star" in the sense of celebrity, like fame and recognition. It was the fact that so much of the creative process of the film seemed to be centered around them. They were very important to the whole operation and responsible for creating much of what was going to finally be on screen. They worked intimately with the director, the producers knew their names, and the guys from the Muppets seemed to be great friends with them. It seemed like an amazing privilege. They were living my dream.

Being so young, inexperienced, and insecure, I was in awe, envious, and intimidated by their presence. I would look at them and wonder what kind of person you had to be to be a Teenage Mutant Ninja Turtle. Over time, I was to discover many different answers to that question, but one thing I can tell you for sure, you mostly have to be the kind of person that's under five foot seven.

MEET THE TURTLES

Leif Tilden was the compact, blonde-haired performer from New York that played Donatello. A lot of people on the film were from New York because Henson did a lot of casting there and would audition local performers who could handle the rigors of costume suit work.

Leif was quirky. He looked like a California surf kid and had a very unique voice; like he had a cold and was sucking on helium at the same time. Leif told me he was one of the voices of the M&M's in a commercial once. Leif was quick witted and cocky with a sense of the artist about him. To me, he seemed really cool. Leif was the kind of guy that I desperately wanted to like me, and I wanted to be like; kind of like Val Kilmer in the movie *Real Genius*. Unfortunately, I tried too hard to make Leif like me, which is not an uncommon occurrence in my life. By trying hard to prove to him that I was witty and quirky like him, I was really not being myself. I was even more awkward than if I had just remained true to myself and that resulted in a clumsy relationship with Leif. In addition, at times, Leif's sense of humor could even be a little sharp, so if you were insecure like me, it was easy to take things personally. I eventually surmised that Leif's cocky manner and drive to be witty may have been dedicated efforts to try and cover what might be his own insecurities.

Michelin Sisti ("Meesh'-uh-lin Sis'-tee") was the dark-haired, elfin performer who portrayed Michelangelo. Micha ("Meesh-a"), or "Meesh," as we called him, was truly a dear, dear man. I have spent only a small portion of my life around him, on the film set and at a couple of comic-cons, but I love him. I have never seen Micha say "no" to anybody for anything. He comes across as being *grateful* to be in *your* presence. During the first film, Micha was in his early forties and the oldest of the turtle performers. Micha occasionally smoked cigarettes at that time, so when he was in his turtle suit, he used one of those old fashioned, long, skinny cigarette holders, like in movies from the 1940's, to reach in through the turtle mouth. It reached back all the way through the turtle mask so he could puff away in between takes without taking off his head. It was funny to see Michelangelo smoking from an elegant cigarette holder and then exhaling a cloud of smoke from his turtle mouth. Micha can actually be seen in the first film as the Domino's Pizza delivery guy who passes the pizza through the sewer to himself as Mikey.

David Forman played Leonardo. Dave was English and was an accomplished tumbler who represented England in the 1980 World Games. After that, he was hired by the famous special effects designer Rick Baker to play an ape in the movie *Greystoke: The Legend of Tarzan*. Because the Henson organization was originally looking for suit performers in London, where the turtle technical and wardrobe components were being developed, Dave was a local and was able to participate early in the process of helping to develop the suits. Dave seemed rather quiet, at least during the times I was around him. He didn't seem to me to really interact with the other guys as much, but then again, I wasn't part of their everyday group on this film.

Raphael was played by Josh Pais. Josh was a Jewish guy, about 5' 7" and 29 years old, with curly brown hair. Of all the actors, despite him being a few years older, Josh and I were the most similar. Josh has the distinction of being the only actor in the Ninja Turtles films to have both worn the costume and supplied the voice for his own character. He can be seen in the first movie as "Passenger in Cab" when Raphael rolls over the taxi hood while chasing Casey Jones out of Central Park. Josh is the guy in the back seat of the taxi that says, "What the heck was that?"

I remember watching these four guys work and thinking different things. First of all, they looked sweaty and miserable when they were in the turtle suits, but that seemed like a small price to pay for being such an important part of making a big-time movie. Second of all, I thought there was no reason I couldn't be doing what they were doing. I just needed a chance.

ACTION!

After a couple of weeks of rehearsal, all the sets were completed and we started shooting the movie; going from pre-production, into production, or principal photography. The way the Ninja Turtles film worked was that we shot two units simultaneously. We had one complete filmmaking unit, directed by Steve Barron, which filmed all the scenes with the main actors and puppeteers performing the lines from the script and also some action. We also had a second unit, directed by Brian Henson, Jim Henson's son, that shot some action scenes, pick-up shots, and the flashbacks to the turtles as babies in the sewer. "Pick-up shots" are when you realize that you forgot to shoot something important on the day you were filming, so you go back later and get whatever you need to make a scene work. In other words, you go back and "pick up" what you missed.

With two units, the Ninja Turtle film crews could shoot simultaneously on different sets and get a whole lot more movie shot in a very short time. In some instances, we would shoot action for part of the day with the stunt turtles, then the first unit with the actor turtles would come in and fill in the dialogue moments during the fight. For instance, in one scene, Michelangelo spins around to knock out a Foot Soldier, then looks up and says, "I love being a turtle!" In a scene like that, the stunt turtle, Wil, might perform the actual fight before lunch, then after lunch, first unit would come in and Micha would stand in the correct spot, do the very last part of the martial arts move, and then say the line. It was a constant game of shooting back and forth like that throughout the film.

When the first unit came in and took over the sets, it was quite a production in and of itself, like watching the circus come to town.

First, the puppeteers rumbled in, with their team of assistants wheeling in the large industrial cases with the robotic controls.

Mak Wilson was the puppeteer for Michelangelo. Mak was a petite guy and got his start doing suit work in *The Dark Crystal* most notably as one of the Mystics. He would go on to be the lead puppeteer in the hit movie *Babe*, (you know, Babe, that adorable movie about the pig that wins the dog show. Sorry if that was a spoiler.)

Marty Robinson did the puppetry for Leonardo. Marty had also been Mr. Snuffleupagus on *Sesame Street*.

David Rudman was the puppeteer for Donatello. David would go on later to perform as Cookie Monster.

Finally, David Greenaway did the puppetry for Raphael. David was an interesting guy whom I would get to know even better on the second film. On this one, he was just a dark, mysterious Englishman, and by dark, I mean he seemed like a poet who drank a lot and mourned lost love. David would eventually go on to work with Frank Oz helping perform Yoda for various *Star Wars* films.

Behind the puppeteers came Leif, David, Josh, and Micha in their wondrous green, foam-rubber suits. Because a whole human being is inside each costume, when you stand next to them, each turtle actually has a slightly larger-than-life feel, like miniature, muscular, green astronauts in flight suits and backpacks.

Each turtle actor was accompanied by a "dresser," the person responsible for getting them into the turtle suit in the morning and then taking care of their needs, and the costume, throughout the day.

In addition to the turtles, sometimes their teacher, Splinter the rat, would also make an appearance. Unlike the turtles, Splinter was not a costume, he was actually a full puppet, operated by a puppeteer's hand and arm thrust all the way up into his head. The puppeteer had an assistant and support crew to help control and care for the entire creature. The main puppeteer responsible for Splinter was Kevin Clash. Kevin was awesome to be around and a very sweet and friendly guy. When I first encountered Splinter on set, Kevin was doing Splinter's voice in the low, throaty timber that you actually hear in the movie. A few days later, I heard another voice come out of Kevin...a voice that haunted me...the voice of Elmo, the little red puppet from *Sesame Street* who loves everybody. Kevin was Splinter and Elmo!

Holy cow!

I hated Elmo. But, we each have our cross to bear.

Along with all the puppets and Henson support staff in first unit, there was a whole host of grip, electric, make-up, wardrobe, and production personnel filling out the rest of the massive crew.

The last people to come to set were always the actual human actors, like Elias Koteas and Judith Hoag.

Judith was super sweet. She really showed genuine concern for the actors and the pain and suffering they were going through in the costumes during the long, hot shoot days. She was very protective of them, just like April would be of the turtles. She complained to the producers and advocated quite vehemently to make sure the actors were taken care of and given opportunities to rest and recuperate during the tedious periods of filming. I've since been to several comic-cons with Judith and am always really moved by how genuine and kind she is.

One other guy I really liked was Ray Serra, the actor who played "Chief Sterns," the high-strung New York police chief. Ray was a short guy with a big New York personality. He called everybody "baby," saying, "Great to meet you, baby," and "See you later, baby." It didn't matter if you were a guy or a girl.

If the Shredder was involved in a scene, then actor James Saito would arrive. He had been in pretty much every television show ever from the late '70s on. What was really cool was seeing the Shredder's costume up close, like a samurai Darth Vader. His helmet was awesome, a combination of fiberglass and metal. His costume was made out of a similar material as the Foot costumes, but red instead of black. It was a coarse fabric woven with little silver threads throughout. I'm not sure what it's supposed to look like on screen, whether it be armor or chainmail or something, but I always see it for the odd synthetic material that it was.

The real badass among the actors was Toshishiro Obata. He played Tatsu, the Shredder's main lieutenant. Toshishiro Obata is a real Aikido and sword master with genuine samurai lineage. Obata Sensei, as Pat called him on the set, did not speak much, but when he did, you listened, and you listened very hard in order to break through his heavy accent. Although he seemed rather stern, he enjoyed a good time, laughed a lot, and even came out to a local bar once in a while with the rest of the Foot Soldiers.

Once all the crew was in place and the actors were ready to shoot, sometimes the production had to wait on all the turtle parts to work. There was a lot of technology being used for the turtles and when you count up all the different motors that had to work, and add in all the different mechanical and digital controls that had to function precisely, you realize it was amazing that the Henson guys were able to keep all that stuff working throughout the duration of filming at all. There's a lot of tiny stuff that can go wrong with all those different parts and it happened quite often. Sometimes faces did not work, servos burned out, signals weren't being transmitted, or controls broke. When this happened, it might be a quick fix, or it could be hours before they got things functioning as they needed to.

If one turtle wasn't working correctly through remote control, they would run hard wires from the puppet controls, across the soundstage, and up the turtle's leg, into the head. Other times, if a broken head belonged to a turtle that wasn't speaking in the scene, the director would just tell them to turn their heads away from camera or stand behind another turtle and discreetly hide their face.

THE BEAT GOES ON

The early part of shooting went on and I spent my first days as a member of the Foot Clan working on the fight choreography. On days that they shot action, we were being used a lot, and it was super exciting and fun. On other days, when it was mostly about the actors working with first unit for dialogue scenes, we had a lot of time to kill.

With so much time when we weren't being used, we hung around our soundstage, or "Foot Headquarters," waiting. At first, we did a lot of rehearsing and working on the fights, but once we had that stuff down we looked for other activities to occupy our time. We spent a lot of time playing stick ball inside the sound stage. The building was so big, it was like our own little domed stadium. Some of us took advantage of the time and equipment around us to practice stunt falls into pads. A lot of the Foot Soldiers used their downtime to work out.

Because there were so many martial artists working on the film, it wasn't too long each day before one guy might start leading an impromptu seminar on some obscure martial arts technique, or guys might start pairing off and working out together on their own stuff. I remember one guy named Rudy. He was a real Southern boy, out of the back country of North Carolina somewhere. He was watching some of the guys work out and started bragging a little and challenging some of them to meet him on our day off and match him and his buddies in their particular workout. When

103

one of the guys asked Rudy what kind of workout he and his buddies did, Rudy responded in his thick Southern accent, and in no uncertain terms, "Man, we run through da woods." I wasn't sure if this was some kind of incredible ninja training technique, or just something he and his buddies did to practice getting away from the moonshine cops.

Pat Johnson was in his early 50's at the time we made the Ninja Turtle movie and was an avid workout-aholic. He only ate one meal a day, lunch, and he would eat as much as he wanted. When Pat wasn't needed for work duties, he would spend his time doing Sudoku puzzles, reading, or exercising. He always had boxing gloves and focus mitts with him and would get his assistant Barbara to hold the pads while he slammed away. He was in great shape, was a very accomplished martial artist, and had an amazing intensity about him.

When it came to exercising, a couple of us would join Pat on his daily workouts and contribute various exercises that we thought might be challenging for each other. For instance, we would prop ourselves between two chairs and do dips and push-ups. We would secure a broomstick between the two chair backs and do pull ups, and lots of sit-ups. The core workout group was Pat, kickboxing champion Dale "Sunshine" Frye, Billy Liu (the Hong Kong stunt-man), and me. Our workouts were a lot of fun and we would challenge each other to see who could do the most reps.

Sometimes while working out, if there happened to be a lot of extras on set that day, some of them would amble over and watch. I remember one time, one of the young guys playing a gang member in the Shredder's headquarters was watching us and lit up a cigarette nearby. As soon as Pat smelled it he let loose on the kid; "Get that fuckin' thing out of here you fucking asshole! What the fuck are you thinking?" The kid backed away immediately. Pat hated smoking.

Eventually, after the first movie, Pat would take many of the exercises he did with the chairs and use them as a starting point to develop an exercise device called the "Grab-Bar." It looked like a runner's hurdle with handles so that you could do push-ups, dips, modified pull-ups, leg raises, etc. I loved it and bought two; one for me and one for my mom. She used hers to hang clothes.

Outside of the physical pastimes, one of the things that was the most fun to do was play cards with the Hong Kong stunt guys. They taught us a game called "Cho Dai Di" which basically means "The Big Two." It's like a Chinese poker game, similar to Crazy Eights, the object being to get rid of all your cards first. It was addicting. I mean really addicting. It's fast-paced and really easy to learn. Once a small group of us learned to play, there was always a game going on somewhere. Instead of playing for money, as is traditionally done, we played so that the loser had to do push-ups for all the points left in their hands. My friends and I would continue to play this game for many years and I still play it with family members and friends today.

BRUSHES WITH GREATNESS

One of the other things I did when we had down time was explore the movie lot. They were filming other movies there at the same time, so there was no telling what or who you might be able to see. The movie lot was fairly big, with multiple soundstages, so everybody pretty much stayed out of everybody else's way, and you could easily go for days without actually encountering anyone from another film. One of those other films on the lot was *The Exorcist 3*.

One day we were on a lunch break. It was hot outside and most of the Foot Soldiers wanted to kick back in the air conditioning of the soundstage. I didn't care about the heat, I was excited about exploring the movie lot, so I took advantage of the time and trotted across the studio towards the backlot. I wanted to look around the fake New York city street, the same one I saw the last year when I snuck onto the lot in the pizza uniform. This time they were going to use the backlot for the exterior of April's New York apartment building and I wanted to see what they were constructing.

On the way, I passed the trailers and soundstage of the Exorcist film. There was nobody around because everybody was inside working. But just as I walked past one of the trailers, the door swung open, and out stepped the famous actor George C. Scott. He was a guy I saw in movies growing up and watched in film

106

school. He was an institution of American acting, in films like *Anatomy of a Murder* and *Dr. Strangelove.*

He started walking towards the soundstage right in front of me, and more than anything, I wanted to talk to him, or touch him, or engage with him in some way. I just wanted to interact with him for a moment. He was the biggest star I had ever seen in my life; the rest of my experience being limited to getting the autographs of country singer Charlie Pride and my local weatherman at a pro-am golf tournament when I was 12. Thoughts scrambled through my brain as I tried to think of something to say. I remembered the amazing opening speech he made in his Academy Award-winning performance in *Patton,* and I thought about his turn as the sinister Bert Gordon in *The Hustler* with Paul Newman. He was amazing. So many great performances, so much material to choose from. So, I said...

"It sure is hot, huh?"

He nodded and kept walking, and then, without even turning around, he said, "It's fucking bullshit." Then he disappeared inside the stage door.

What a day!

A couple of days later, I was making a similar trip around the lot, figuring maybe I would see him again, and I passed by another set of trailers near another soundstage. As I passed one of the trailers, I heard the sounds of an electric bass guitar. It wasn't really a song I heard, more like sporadic notes played in no particular order.

At that time, besides making movies, my favorite thing to do was play music, still is really. My brother and I spent our high school and college years playing in garage bands and writing music. So, as I heard these low bass notes wailing out of the trailer, I couldn't help but peer into the open door to see who was playing. I looked in and saw a guy sitting on a couch with a black bass guitar on his lap.

It was Keanu Reeves.

I couldn't remember if he was "Bill" or "Ted" in their "Excellent Adventure," but I knew he was a new, young movie star.

"Hey," I said.

"Hey," he replied.

"I heard you playing the bass and just figured I'd see what was going on."

Keanu held up a shiny black bass guitar, "Yeah, I just got this."

I smiled, "Wow, very cool! I play a little bit, too."

He held the guitar out to me and said, "Well, maybe you can show me something. C'mon in." I entered the trailer and sat down next to him. He handed me the instrument.

I wasn't really that good a bass player, but I was good at one particular bass line, for Chuck Berry's *Johnny B. Goode*.

"I know this," I said, and I proceeded to hammer out the song.

Keanu leaned forward, "Hey, that is awesome. Can you show me how it goes?"

For the next 10 minutes, I gave Keanu Reeves a bass guitar lesson.

True story.

And Keanu was as sweet and nice as he could be.

THE LETTER

Having gotten a job as a special abilities extra, the next big step for me was trying to figure out how to turn my current employment situation into a further chance to get my Screen Actors Guild card. It would be a huge step in helping me before I moved to Los Angeles to pursue my full-fledged career. I figured I would ask Pat Johnson about it and see if he could help me. He had gotten to know me a little better through all the choreography work and our workouts together, and he was acting very much like a father-figure to me and all the Foot.

I decided to write Pat a letter.

It took me a few days to write it. This was before the internet and email and all that. I wrote it on a yellow legal pad and filled several pages before typing it up. The letter explained my dreams and aspirations to move to Los Angeles and pursue a career in film. I pointed out that there were a lot of local martial artists working on the film who had wives, kids, and jobs; many were doing it for the great experience and then would go back to their regular lives. But, a few of us were seeing this as a first step towards bigger things. I explained to Pat my whole background and my desire to get the coveted SAG card. I ended it by saying, if there was anything he could do to help me pursue my goals, I would greatly appreciate it. It was overly written, but I felt compelled to let it all hang out.

I felt as if all my hopes were tied up in that letter. By giving it to Pat, I would either embarrass myself and just continue things on my own, or he might be able to help by wielding his all-powerful hand among the gods of Hollywood. I felt anxious about handing it to him myself, thinking I would probably say something stupid, so I delivered the letter to his hotel and let them give it to him. I felt an amazing amount of anxiety dropping it off, as if I had written to Santa requesting my dream.

A couple of days went by and Pat didn't say anything. Neither did I. If he wasn't going to bring it up, I sure wasn't. Then one day, Pat walked up to me and said, "Kenn, I want you to know I got your letter. It was very good." Then he walked away.

I think I might have had a little orgasm.

TALKATIVE FOOT #2

Over the next couple of days, we were going to shoot scenes 87-93, inside April's apartment, when Raphael crashes through the skylight and the Foot Clan come pouring in after him. It's the most elaborate fight of the film. In this scene, Nam, the stunt performer from Hong Kong, was dressed as Raph and threw himself through the skylight, landing in a stack of cardboard boxes below. I followed him down as a Foot Soldier, jumping through the broken glass with Tom DeWier, and landing in the same boxes. At this point, Raph is unconscious and the three other turtles have to take on the entire ninja gang.

I played several different Foot Soldiers in this scene, including jumping through the skylight, swinging through the windows, and being the "fellow 'chucker" in the duel with Michelangelo.

For the fellow 'chucker moment, I had worked with the prop-master to find the right pair of nunchakus. To start, they gave me a pair of heavy wooden ones that were hard to spin around quickly. He tried to make them lighter by drilling out the handles, but they were still too heavy and slow, not to mention dangerous. Instead, they gave me a pair made out of PVC pipe with a thin layer of black foam rubber on the outside and a black chord holding them together. These were super light and I could whip them around really fast. After an initial camera test, they felt (I am vainly proud to say) that the movements of the dark sticks were too fast for the camera to pick up. To remedy that, they painted a silver stripe

111

down each handle that would help the camera see them, as if the silver stripe was a reflection of light.

The object of the scene was for me to look good as the bad guy, but for Michelangelo to look even better as the hero. In order for that to happen, Wil, the stuntman playing Mikey, spent a lot of time working with the nunchakus while wearing the turtle suit. The foam rubber hands and the large shell on his back made it especially challenging to do anything amazing. Because it was easier for me to do nunchaku tricks in a ninja outfit than it was for Wil to do them in a thick, foam latex turtle suit, I ended up looking like more of a badass in the scene. They wanted Wil to be more impressive, so they had to figure out how to accomplish that.

They cut a hole in the end of his turtle glove and ran some clutch cable down from the glove to the leg, and out to a power drill just below camera. They mounted a stiff set of nunchakus onto the end of the clutch cable at his fingertip. When the prop master activated the drill, the clutch cable spun around and made the nunchakus spin like an airplane propeller. That was never in the original script, it was just something they came up with because they had to make Mikey look better. It turned out to be a very funny moment as well.

Right after that moment happens, there's another moment in the script when one of the Foot Soldiers pulls out a sword and says to Donatello, "I'm going to turn you into turtle soup. But first, I'm going to shell you like an oyster." Then he proceeds to get his ass kicked by Donatello. That part was listed in the script as "Talkative Foot #2." Talkative Foot #2 was going to be played by Tom DeWier, the young stunt man that Pat brought with him from Los Angeles. Tom was not considered a "special abilities extra" like the rest of us, making only $75 per day; he was actually hired to work on the film under a SAG contract as a "utility stunt performer," and he was being paid whatever the SAG union rate was at that time for stunts, probably about $1600-$1750 per week. "Utility stunt performer" means Tom could be used over and over to play various characters without requiring separate contracts to do it. He was there to do anything the producers needed him to do throughout the movie, like play a Foot Soldier, or double the Shredder. Now, the producers also wanted Tom to be Talkative Foot #2 so they wouldn't have to pay someone else to do it.

Things didn't necessarily work out like they planned.

The morning of the shoot, Pat Johnson approached me and said, "Kenn, I need you to do something for me."

I snapped to attention, "Of course, Pat, what do you need?"

He said, "Walk with me, my son," and stepped outside the soundstage. I followed obediently.

As we stepped into the morning sunlight, Pat said, "We're supposed to film a scene today with a talking Foot Soldier. Tom was supposed to play the role, but he's sick today, so we need somebody to take his place. If the director says you're okay, I want you to do it...and that will get you your SAG card."

My jaw hit the ground.

The very thing I had asked Pat to help me with in my letter was happening, right then, right there. He was offering me a chance to get my SAG card and overcome what was presumably the first and most difficult challenge of breaking into the movies (besides being talented). I was dumbfounded.

"Pat, thank you so much," I said.

"Don't thank me," he replied, "Just do a good job." Pat then handed me the sides for the part. "Sides" are excerpts of a script, just a few pages stapled together. Each actor, the producer, the director, and many other crew members get a set of sides from the 2nd AD each morning. The sides let them know exactly what scenes, action, and dialogue are being shot that day. Pat pointed out my part on the page and said, "Lemme hear you do it."

I said the lines out loud for Pat, deliberately enunciating each syllable with, what I believed to be, a Japanese accent. I figured I was a ninja, so I was probably from Japan like my boss, Shredder, right?

Pat looked up, "What the hell are you doing?"

"What do you mean?" I asked.

Pat grabbed the sides, "What's all this 'I—am—going—to—turn—you- bullshit?" He said the words with the same deliberate emphasis on every syllable as I had.

"You need to get tough with it," he said.

Pat started breathing heavily through his nose, snorting in and out, swaying his shoulders like a boxer. He gritted his teeth and glared at me. When he spoke, he sounded like a New York thug from a 1940s gangster film, "I'm gunna toin ya into toitle soup. But first, I'm gonna shell ya like an oystuh!" He let out his breath and handed me back the sides, "Now you try it, like that."

I did as he asked, softening some of the Brooklyn-ese, but speaking as if I was saying it myself, not as some pretend villain from the Far East.

Pat nodded, "Okay, good. Let's go see the director."

We walked across the lot into one of the other sound stages. I couldn't believe Pat Johnson was escorting me into the inner sanctum of first unit.

The director, Steve Barron, was busy shooting dialogue between April and the turtles in the apartment before the big fight starts. I stood quietly by Pat and watched the actors and puppeteers working in tandem. At their next break in filming, Pat spoke with the assistant director who brought the director over. Pat addressed him, "Hi Steven. As you know, we've had to replace our talking Foot for today, I thought Kenn would be a great replacement."

The director smiled, "Oh, excellent."

All nearby eyes turned to me.

Steve said, "Anytime you're ready, please do the lines."

I started snorting and puffing like Pat had done and launched into the scene, giving it my all, heeding Pat's earlier direction not to sound like an idiot pretending to be Japanese. When I was done, the director nodded his head, "Ok, very good. Thank you. That'll do fine." Then he turned and walked back to the set.

Pat turned to me with a smile, "Good job." Then he headed towards the door with me in tow, smiling from ear to ear.

I was now Talkative Foot #2!

We headed back to the Foot headquarters to gather the rest of the fighters for a full day of filming the action.

The day quickly escalated into a whirlwind of activity. We were shooting the most complex fight in the film, starting from the moment Raph crashes through the skylight, to the end of the fight when April, the Turtles, and Casey Jones escape from the burning antique store below the apartment. It was over several days that we shot all the fight segments we had been creating and practicing during the previous weeks.

Today, when I watch the film with my friends or at comic-cons with fans, during this scene, every few seconds I point at different Foot Soldiers and shout, "That's me!"

Here's a list of a few of the more visible things that I got to do:
- I jump down through the broken skylight into the apartment.
- I swing on the ropes and crash through the windows.
- I do the nunchaku spin-off with Mikey.
- I get flipped in the kitchen and crash to the floor.
- I call for the battle axes, screaming "Bisentos, now!"
- I chop the battle axe into the floor, chasing the turtle across the kitchen.

Eventually, when we got to the "turtle soup" scene with Talkative Foot #2, the director called me over and asked, "Kenn, are you ready?"

115

I nodded, "Definitely."

We spent 15 or 20 minutes filming that scene and getting a few different camera angles. Because Donatello has some lines in that moment, we shot the scene with me facing off against Leif Tilden, the turtle actor for Donnie. For a brief few minutes, my fantastic dreams were coming to complete fruition. I was an important part of the action taking place on set. Sure, the fellow 'chucker scene was cool, but this time I actually had lines and my pay grade was a lot higher, I was getting a SAG daily contract to play the part, making about $450 for the day. This was one of those cases where the director needed me to do the part, so the producers did the paperwork and got me accepted into the Screen Actors Guild. Now I could say lines in the movie. It was a huge milestone!

The mic was positioned to pick up my voice, the wardrobe department fussed over my uniform to make sure it was perfect, the director knew my name! It was super exciting and a thrill when he called "Action!"

I delivered my lines a few times and then got punched out by Donnie, over and over. They repositioned the camera to make sure they got it from all the necessary angles. Each time the director shouted "Action," my heartbeat jumped with excitement.

I didn't want it to end. But we eventually got it in the can and the production had to move on. I returned to join the rest of the Foot soldiers and Pat gave me a big thumbs-up.

"Good job, my son," he said.

I smiled big.

I was to find out later, when everything was said and done, the scene was actually cut from the final film. And it wasn't because of my performance. I know they didn't cut it because of lousy acting on my part, they could have easily dubbed my lines from behind the mask with a superior actor. They actually dubbed all of Tatsu's lines in the movie, and he wasn't even wearing a mask. I eventually found out that they cut the scene because it slowed down the action overall, it was too much conversation in the middle of the excitement of the big fight. But it didn't matter, I still got my SAG card.

The day we shot, I also ended up being the Foot Soldier that calls for the battle axes and says the line, "Bisentos, now!" That is actually my voice screaming for the battle axes. By having me do that part that day too, the producers saved money on hiring somebody else for saying just those two words. No matter how you looked at it, I was kicking ninja ass.

HONG KONG PHOOEY

When we finally finished filming that big fight, I was feeling great because I had gotten to do a lot of gags ("gag" is movie lingo for a stunt). I had spent a lot of time working with the stunt turtles and actor turtles, the director knew my name, and Pat Johnson was happy with my work.

Luckily, he wasn't the only one.

I was approached by Venus Wong. Venus was from Hong Kong and was in charge of managing and taking care of the Chinese stunt team. Venus told me that Mo, the stunt double for Leonardo, wanted to speak to me and she asked if I could take a walk with them.

A few minutes later, the three of us marched to the backlot and sat down on a curb. Mo did not speak any English so Venus translated. "He says he like your martial art and movement very much."

I bowed my head slightly, "Tell him, thank you very much. I am honored to work with him and learn from him, too."

She translated and he smiled and uttered, "Thank you."

Venus continued, "He say he like to offer you job working in movies in Hong Kong. Come be stuntman, work with his team."

What? Holy crap! Are you kidding me? He just offered me a job...in Hong Kong...in the movies! In kung-fu movies! Holy crap!

She continued, "He pay you $2,000 a month."

The money didn't sound like a lot, only a quarter of a SAG contract, but it was something. "Thank you very much," I said. "I am very honored."

I didn't ask for too many details, I was just thrilled he was asking me. But, I immediately had some doubts in my head about whether I wanted to do something like this. Up to this point, everything I was doing in America to become a movie star had been working out, and it seemed like leaving the country for so little money would undermine my goal.

I bowed my head again and said, "Is it okay for me to think about it and give an answer later?"

Venus translated for Mo. He nodded and she responded. "He says yes, but please tell him soon so he can make phone call to Hong Kong."

We got up, shook hands and went back to join the rest of the crew.

At this time, I had very little experience in the film business and definitely no world travel or cultural experience. I was an ignorant kid figuring stuff out as I went along, stumbling occasionally, but also finding my way to some successes. This question of whether to take this job or not required wisdom beyond my years and experience.

I went to David Chan, the Chinese producer of the film. I told him the deal Mo offered me. He laughed.

"Don't do it," he said. "Only do it if they offer you a million dollars."

That seemed like a lot of money. I asked why and he said, "Because you will get to Hong Kong and, if you get hurt, they will leave you outside on the street and lock the gate behind you. They will act like they don't know you. Then you will be hurt and stuck in Hong Kong."

I took every word he said as gospel and it put some fear into me. I didn't want to end up hurt, lying in the street in Hong Kong. That sounded awful.

It's at this point that I can look back and realize that two things occurred which shaped my destiny from that point forward; 1) David Chan had no idea that he was giving me advice that would influence the very direction of my life, and 2) I was an idiot kid who had no idea how to handle the real world.

So, here's what happened…

The next day, Venus and Mo approached me.

"Do you have decision?" she asked.

"Yes," I said confidently, "Tell Mo, I'll do it…for a million dollars."

Her eyes got big. Mo grabbed her arm and asked her to translate. She did and his eyes got big, too. Then he grunted something in Cantonese. "That crazy," she said, "Why you say million dollars?"

I answered with the confidence of a well-informed idiot, "Because if I go there, and if I get hurt, they might put me out on the street, close the gate, and act like they don't know me. Then I'll be hurt and stuck in Hong Kong." I did a great job of parroting what David had said to me. I was also feeling confident that I was on my way to being the next action hero in America already, so I didn't feel like I was losing out on anything.

As you can imagine, my response didn't go over very well. After just a little more talk, Venus and Mo realized that I was sticking to my guns and turned and marched off, shaking their heads.

In all honesty, it's one of the two decisions in my life that I truthfully regret. To this day, I wish I had gone to Hong Kong and experienced the wacky adventure that could have been working in their film industry. Unfortunately, I didn't have the experience or confidence to see the possibilities at the time and make a better, more well-informed decision.

The other thing I wish I had done differently in life was to join the army.

WINS BY A NOSE

After completing the big fight scene, we had a day off before returning to filming and shifting to a nighttime schedule. The change in schedule would allow us to shoot all the exteriors that take place at night in the script. One of those scenes is in Central Park where Raphael chases two purse snatchers and meets Casey Jones for the first time.

The actual interaction between the two main characters was shot in a park in North Carolina, not New York. The scene included Elias Koteas as Casey and Josh Pais as the actor Raphael. At one point, after Raphael criticizes Casey for carrying a "Jose Canseco" bat, Casey pulls out a cricket bat and bashes Raph with it, sending him flying through the air and landing headfirst in a trashcan. The actual original line in the script was, "A Wade Boggs bat?" but I guess at the time Jose Conseco had been in the news for some eccentric behavior and they changed the line on the spot.

Anyway, in order to have Raph land headfirst in the can, they took Nam, the Raph stunt double, hung him upside down by his ankles, and dropped him into the trash can. Unfortunately, an important structural piece inside the turtle head rests right across the bridge of the performer's nose, and when Nam hit the bottom of the trash can, that piece smashed down and broke his nose. Lucky for the crew, they got the shot in one take. Unlucky for Nam, he had to go to the hospital.

The next day, after I got to set, Pat Johnson pulled me aside. "Kenn, I have something I want you to do."

I nodded and said, "Yes, sir." At this point, I would do anything Pat asked of me.

Pat looked as stern and serious as he ever did and said, "Last night during the shoot, Nam had to go to the hospital."

I grimaced, "Oh no, is he okay?" At this point, Nam was my friend, spending our off time together with the other Hong Kong guys, going to the beach, eating out, and all that. I didn't know what had happened and I was concerned for his welfare.

Pat continued, "Yes, he's fine, but he broke his nose and can't wear the Raphael costume anymore. I want you to go to the creature shop. If you can fit into the Raphael suit, you've got to take over for Nam for the rest of the film. You'll be the new stunt Raphael."

It's hard for me to describe the feeling I had at that moment. At that point, I felt bad for Nam's misfortune, but I was also overwhelmed by the good fortune I was having because of it. Pat smiled, "This also means they have to give you a new contract, as well."

He was right. If I became Raphael for the rest of the film, the producers would have to put me on a standard SAG weekly stunt contract, about $1,600-$1,750 a week or so at that time. That's a huge jump from the $75 a day I was making as a Foot Soldier, and a lot more than the $450 I was paid to be "Talkative Foot #2" for a single day. I was ready to bust out of my pants.

Pat quickly brought me back down to earth. "First," he said, "you've gotta fit in the suit."

Pat's assistant Barbara walked me over to the creature shop, a separate building on the movie lot dedicated to the Henson group and all their technology wizards, painters, costumers, et al. I walked in and Barbara presented me to one of the assistant directors who then introduced me to the Henson folks. This is when I first met

William Plant, the Englishman that Jim Henson designated as the "Project Supervisor" for the whole Ninja Turtle undertaking. He was responsible for overseeing all the development and creation of the turtle costumes, both inside and out. He was a tall guy with a full head of floppy dark curls. He welcomed me in and introduced a few helpers.

The first thing they did was have me put on a skintight, full body, white lycra suit. It felt weird to be wearing a unitard in the middle of all these people, but anything for art, right?

They pulled out an assortment of the various Raphael costume parts and then coated me in baby powder to make it easier to slide the foam latex pieces on. They first showed me how to pull on the short foam rubber pants. The costume was originally custom made for Nam who was a very slender guy with probably 3% body fat, a real ectomorph. I on the other hand am a more compact American mesomorph with a lifelong challenge to battle my love of pizza and french fries.

Fortunately, I was in great shape at the time, but it was still a challenge to fit into Nam's suit. Everything was so tight, just barely stretching over my limbs. Then, I slid into the piece that made up the shoulders and upper arms...and it didn't fit. My chest was broader than Nam's, so the piece wouldn't go on correctly. The dressers frowned.

My heart sank.

What I didn't realize was that the people in the creature shop wanted to do everything they could in order to make this work. The producers were desperate to find a replacement and if they had to keep searching for another guy, it might cost them more time and more money.

The dressers went in the next room and came back with spare parts from all the other turtles. I was closest in size to Dave Forman (actor-Leo) and Josh Pais (actor-Raph), so they found body parts

123

from their costumes that could fit me. I squeezed into a set of Leo's shoulders and I even got a pair of Donatello's feet. Slowly but surely, they cobbled together various parts from the different turtles, threw on a Raphael head, and I stood there like a Franken-stein turtle birthed from the limbs of my brothers.

They looked at me and one of the dressers said, "Well, I guess you're the new Raphael."

That moment changed my whole life.

From that point forward, I was forever destined to be known as "the guy that played Raphael." I'm definitely not the only one. There were others before and after me, including Josh, Nam, and other dudes over the next few years, but I was now one of them. Of course, I didn't realize all of this at that moment, but I did realize I had just taken a huge step towards my dreams.

I had just become a Teenage Mutant Ninja Turtle.

NEW YORK, NEW YORK

I spent the rest of the shoot jumping in and out of various scenes as Raphael, including: being on the rooftop right before Raph gets attacked and thrown through the skylight; the training sequences by the farmhouse; the taxi cab scene near Central Park with Casey Jones; the subway fight when Raph saves April from the Foot Soldiers; and various pick-up shots of different scenes to complete any action that was missed.

All the guys from Hong Kong, as well as Ernie, had gotten to know me pretty well at that point, so it was a fairly smooth transition to go from Foot to turtle. I also got a lot of support and celebration from my Foot Soldier brethren. They were excited for me and congratulated me with pats on the back.

It wasn't long after first getting the part of stunt Raphael that Pat informed me that I was to leave for New York.

The entire Ninja Turtle movie takes place in New York, but only a few scenes were actually filmed in the Big Apple, everything else was done in North Carolina. The shots from New York include: Raph leaving the movie theater; Raph running across the street and rolling over the taxi cab; the subway scene in which Raph saves April; and Raph stomping across April's roof as he tries to vent his anger just before he's attacked.

For the scene on April's roof, they found a tall apartment build-ing in the city and I, as Raphael, having just argued with my brother Leonardo, was supposed to kick and punch my way across the roof trying to work out my aggression. The production company actually placed the camera, director, and the entire crew on a totally different building several blocks away while a production assistant stayed with me and the director communicated to us through a walkie-talkie.

Arriving at the building was actually pretty funny. I had gotten dressed in the turtle suit in a room at the hotel. When the production assistant showed up to take us to the van, they covered me with a blanket so nobody could see me or take pictures and potentially spoil the surprise of the movie before it came out. They pushed me through the lobby and shuffled me quickly across the sidewalk to a waiting van, slamming the sliding door behind me. They shuttled us to the location and I repeated the blanket run from the van into the building. Once on the roof, the director gave instructions through the radio.

"Kenn," he said, "you've just had an argument with Leo and now you are up there to work out your anger. Do some kicks and jumps, kind of punching the air and letting out your aggression. Okay?"

I nodded and the production assistant radioed back that we were good to go. I turned to Pat Johnson who was with me.

Pat said, "Are you ready, my son?"

I nodded and he patted me on the back, then he left the rooftop and waited in the stairwell with the wardrobe folks.

I sat under the mask, breathing deeply, looking through the two tiny eye holes and seeing the New York skyline. I started singing the Frank Sinatra song *New York, New York* to myself.

My warbling was interrupted by the PA with the walkie-talkie who told me to get ready. Then we heard "Action" across the radio. The PA ducked below the wall and I shadowboxed my way across the roof.

After the first take, the director radioed over that I needed to appear "quite angry," so I attempted to act out the frustration with greater zeal, including a few cartwheels and some spinning kicks.

126

After a few passes so they could zoom in and out, we got it in the can and it was time to move on.

The following two days in New York were a series of night shoots. The first one was Raph leaving the theater, played by Josh Pais, and then me chasing Casey Jones and rolling over the hood of the taxi.

Getting hit by the taxi was a new experience for me. I had to run across the street, at night, and time it with a moving car that screeched to a halt, so I could roll over the hood...all while wearing a thick, foam rubber suit with almost no vision. Now, there are a lot of stunt guys who can take incredible car hits and slam through windshields or get thrown to the ground in spectacular fashion, but I had never messed around with colliding my body against a moving vehicle. It always seemed like a good idea to avoid that growing up. Fortunately, I was young, energetic, and felt invincible, especially in the thick padded suit, so even though I knew there was some danger involved, I was ready.

The first time we got ready to do it, I was quite anxious. I wasn't really sure how it was all going to work out. I mean, your whole life you're taught to avoid getting hit by cars, but here I was, putting myself purposely into a collision course with one. Pat and I marked out the steps a couple of times and the driver ran the cab into position a few times so we could develop the timing.

Pat asked me, "Okay, Kenn, you ready?"

I told him I was and we made final adjustments to secure the turtle head on tight. Then we all got into position.

The director called action, Pat gave the signal, and the cab launched forward. Then Pat called out, "Now, Kenn!"

I started running across the street, my field of vision extremely limited. I could only see the point of contact on the street we had marked for the gag. I ran towards it with faith that the taxi would hit its mark at the right speed and stop in time. If not, I'd run smack into the side of the moving cab at a full run.

I got closer and could just see the cab coming from the edge of my sightline. I took my last couple of timed steps, bent my knees and projected myself forward, head first. The cab screeched to a halt and I somersaulted across the hood, sliding easily over the slick metal and landing fluidly on the other side, continuing to run across the street. It was perfect!

I got to the other side of the street and the director called "Cut!"

Pat was immediately by my side, "Kenn, everything okay?"

I was breathing too hard to talk. I nodded my big turtle head and gave a thumbs-up. "That was great," he said. "Now, let's do it again."

We shot three or four takes of it.

In the film, it actually doesn't look as incredible or dramatic as it felt doing it. But, it's still pretty cool.

Later in my career, when I talked to other stunt guys, I would puff up my chest and say, "Yeah, I've done a car hit."

SUBWAY SANDWICH

We spent the next night in New York in the subway station shooting the scene where Raphael saves April from the Foot Soldiers. As I said at the beginning of this book, we had been assured that no trains would pass through the station before a certain time in the morning.

The evening started with shooting April, played by Judith Hoag, running into the Foot Soldiers for the first time on the empty subway platform.

When the Foot Clan first surprise her, April says, "Am I behind on my Sony payments?" and Talkative Foot #1 slaps her across the face. She then pulls out Raphael's lost sai to try and defend herself, but the Foot Soldier knocks it away.

The very first shot I did that night was the close-up of Raph's hand reaching out from behind a pillar to pick up the fallen sai. I tried to make my hand as stealthy and dramatic as possible. I believe my hand actually overacted.

Pat then got me together with the local New York guys playing the Foot Soldiers and we worked out the fight, choreographing the action right on the spot. Pat looked at the storyboards and asked me what moves I was comfortable doing in the suit, so we decided on a double jumping front kick and a jump spinning crescent kick along with an elbow smash.

For a short, white Jewish kid, I actually had some pretty good hops. I could touch the rim on a basketball goal, had a super-high

129

flying side kick, and I could get up pretty good when doing jump spinning kicks. Unfortunately, it's not easy to get any height on your jumps when you're wearing the turtle suit, so I struggled to launch myself up in that fight. However, despite the encumbrance, I did okay and Pat was very happy. Just like the taxi cab hit, every time I see this scene in the final film, I think "Man, I barely got off the ground with those kicks." I realized that everything that felt superhuman inside the suit certainly appeared smaller and less impressive on the outside.

The real physical challenge of my night in the subway came in two other moments. The first was lifting Judith Hoag's stunt double off the ground as she pretended to be unconscious; the second was having to run down the tracks with her in my arms. It was exhausting, carrying another 120-pound human and skipping over railroad ties.

After all the fighting and the lifting and the running, it was time to get the last shot of the night and wrap the scene up and go home. The last shot was going to be Raphael coming out from the shadows of the subway tunnel. Even though we shot it last, it happens at the beginning of the scene.

Everybody was tired, it had been a long night of shooting. I was exhausted from working in the suit all night, as well as the effort required to do the fights and lifting and carrying the stunt double. I was taking a moment to catch my breath, when Pat came over and told me to get my head back on and go with the production assistant up into the darkness of the tunnel.

"Yes, sir," I said, raising my weary bones.

Not only can you not see very well while wearing a turtle head, but after just a minute or two of wearing it, all the carbon dioxide you're exhaling gets trapped in the confines of the rubber mask and you start breathing it in, which gets you tired really quickly. I was feeling all of the effects of this, not to mention the air we were breathing in the subway system was already dusty and musty, so it basically sucked. The dresser helped me get the head back on and the production assistant started leading me to the tracks. Along the way, the director, Steve Barron stopped me to give his instructions. He raised his voice to be heard through my rubber head.

"Hello, Kenn, can you hear me? It's Steve."

I nodded and gave him the turtle thumbs up.

"Brilliant," he said, "Just head up into the tunnel, and on action, I want you to emerge from the tunnel in ninja fashion, ninja walk rather stealthy. Is that alright?"

"Yes, sir," I responded, speaking loudly so he could hear me.

"Right," he said, "Off you go then."

And just like that I was blindly following a PA into the bowels of the New York City subway system.

Once we got a little way into the tunnel, the PA said, "Go a bit further until you're out of the light," then he turned around and hustled back towards the platform. I was left in the silence and darkness of the tunnel.

Despite the eerie surroundings and an underlying fear of cannibalistic underground dwellers, I felt well insulated in the thick turtle suit and trudged my way a bit further up the tunnel. I turned around and waited for them to call "action" through the bullhorn.

It was actually quite peaceful to be standing there in absolute silence, hearing only the sound of my breathing in the mask. It gave me a moment to reflect on the journey I had been on, and how I was now standing on a movie set in New York, being an action hero. It was everything I had hoped for over almost a decade. Everything I had done to reach my goal was paying off and I was filled with a deep sense of personal joy.

And then I heard the train coming.

The wind started to blow through the tunnel. The lights came around the distant corner and I could see the round headlamp on the lead car. I had nowhere to turn, I knew I couldn't outrun the train, and there was no way I could get back to the platform before it overtook me and I got squashed.

My heart pounded as the train roared closer, the sound filling the tunnel like the roar of hurricane winds. My mind raced, trying to figure out how this could have happened. Did we spend too long in the subway and the city thought we were finished already? The lights became blinding and the sound deafening. I dropped my arms and thought, "I'm going to die."

In a rush of thunder and wind, the train bore down on me.

Then it passed right by me like a metal hurricane, kicking up dust and dirt in copious amounts.

The lighted windows on the train allowed me to see that there was another set of express tracks just a few feet away, separated from me by support beams from floor to ceiling. The train roared by and rolled past the station on those express tracks.

I just about pissed myself.

It was closer than I ever wanted to be to a speeding train and my legs were shaking. I thought, "Thank God...but holy fucking shit, somebody could have warned me this was going to happen." I was pissed off.

But then I heard the screech of a bullhorn and the assistant director called "Okay, Kenn, Action!" I gathered my wits and made my way out of the tunnel on some very shaky legs. Luckily, we got the shot in just one take.

When the scene was over, I shared my experience with Pat and the crew. They thought it was funny as hell.

I did not.

They didn't even use that shot in the film.

132

MARTINI SHOT

After my near death experience in the New York subway, we returned to North Carolina and shot all the training sequences at the farm house, after Raphael heals up. This was basically all the stunt turtles jumping, kicking, and sparring together in the fields. It was mostly us just making up different fight patterns and practice sequences with each other on the spot.

It was hot as hell those days because it was September in North Carolina with incredibly high humidity. There's actually a photograph of me, Mo (*Leo*), and Ernie Reyes, Jr. wearing our turtle costumes, without the heads on, showing how hot and sweaty we were after one of the scenes. I remember distinctly, Ernie said, "Let's take a picture so we can remember how miserable we are right now." We did and, sure enough, when people see it they say, "Man, you guys look miserable." Well done, Ernie.

Those training sequences were pretty much the last thing that we shot for the movie. After that, they wrapped everybody, ("wrapped" means the movie is finished, like "wrap it up").

Then it was time for goodbyes.

One thing about working on a movie is that you become incredibly close with your co-workers. You spend 12-14 hours a day with these people, six days a week, for a few months, sharing an amazing common experience. Although I would not compare anything to the horrors of real war, finishing a film is like having gone to battle together. You end up forming deep bonds and intense friendships with your colleagues. Every film I've ever worked on since then, it's the same thing, but this first turtle film was my first experience of it all.

It's a very bittersweet experience for the film to come to an end. On the one hand, you're excited and happy to see the film completed so it can make its way to theaters, but on the other hand, the opportunity to do what you love in a challenging industry is something you want to keep going in perpetuity, not wanting to worry about where your next gig is going to come from. For me, I knew I was on my way to bigger and better things and I was ready to go make those things happen, so the film coming to an end, as sad as it was, just meant I could keep blazing my own trail forward.

As we were all getting ready to depart and go our separate ways, Pat Johnson approached me and said, "Kenn, you've done some really good work here. I want you to stay by your phone. They are already talking about making another one of these and if they do, you're going to do all the action for Raphael again. Would you like that?"

I couldn't believe it, Pat was already offering me a job, if a sequel got made.

"I would love that, Pat. Thank you," I said.

He nodded, "Let's keep in touch."

Pat became one of the mentors of my life. He taught me so much during that first film and he would go on to help me throughout the early part of my career with opportunities, lessons, and guidance. I even came to discover that Tom DeWier was never sick that day he was supposed to film "Talkative Foot #2." Based on my letter to Pat and all the talking we had done, he worked it out with Tom to call in sick that particular day so I could get my SAG card.

I love you Pat! And you too, Tom!

Everybody on the cast and crew exchanged goodbyes, promising to keep in touch like movie people always do. My roommate Steve and I packed up our meager belongings and drove the four hours back to Greensboro to figure out our next steps. We both wanted to move to Hollywood, but there were other factors to consider. The first consideration was figuring out how we were going to pay for the damage we did to the rented moving van that we slammed into the overhang of a gas station on our way home. Idiots.

I told Steve that it made sense for me to hang out in North Carolina for a bit and see if they were going to make a sequel. In the meantime, I hadn't made a whole lot of money on the first film and needed to figure out a way to build up my bank account, especially after paying $1000 to fix that stupid van. I made a few thousand dollars on the movie, but I also used that money to live the whole summer and pay rent, so my bank account was pretty low. Steve also thought it was a good idea to spend a bit of time making some more money since he had been working as a PA for peanuts. We both decided to find jobs in Greensboro for a couple of months.

My mom had a bedroom in her house I could use, so what little bit of stuff I had was packed up into a few boxes and put in her attic for storage. This included the things I saved from the movie, including the script, a pair of turtle hands from my costume that I snuck out, as well as my Foot mask. I also took the stunt pads I was given to wear under my Foot costume, including knee & elbow pads, forearm & shin pads, and an official crew jacket with an amazing embroidery of the turtles on the back.

I put them in a box like a little treasure chest of turtle memories.

HEY MOVIE STAR, GET ME SOME BUTTER

I figured the fastest and easiest way to make more money while I waited in North Carolina was to be a waiter. It was also probably a good skill to have when moving to L.A. Truth be told, I never actually thought I would have to be a waiter in L.A because I knew I was destined to continue my rocket ship to action stardom, but in the meantime, I had to do something to make money. I saw in the newspaper that a brand-new restaurant was opening nearby. It was called the Village Inn.

I interviewed, got hired, and trained as a waiter for two days, and I hated it. At the end of the second night I knew three things; one, I could never be a waiter; two, restaurant customers are horrible to deal with; and three, because the restaurant was brand new, the manager was having trouble getting food to the tables on time in an organized fashion.

At the end of that night, ready to quit the waiting game, I approached the manager, Brad, and convinced him that I could replace him in the kitchen as the guy that expedites all the food for the wait staff. Being an expediter means you stay in the kitchen and make sure all the dishes prepared by the kitchen staff match what's on the waiters' checks, then you organize them on trays, make sure they are presented/garnished correctly, and get someone to run the food out to the table. I loved that job. It got even better when I realized I could give some cheese sticks or french fries to the bartenders and they would keep my giant plastic cup filled all night long with vodka and soda. I got pretty drunk expediting that food and had a great time. One night I got really drunk and asked the manager for a raise...and he gave it to me.

It wasn't necessarily glamorous to be working in a restaurant kitchen after working on a real movie set, but I needed to make money and save as much as I could. Plus, I was having a lot of fun and really just biding my time, waiting to see if another turtle movie would launch. In the meantime, I was getting my first taste of being a low-grade celebrity.

Friends and family knew about my recent adventures and word got out to the community. The Greensboro city newspaper reached out and did a story. A television reporter from the local CBS news came to the house with a crew and interviewed me. Even my old high school newspaper put me on the cover. My mom, who is a well-respected interior designer, got excited when she got a call from a reputable trade publication who wanted to do a story on her. When she returned the call, she found out they actually wanted to do a story about "The designer's son who became a Teenage Mutant Ninja Turtle." She took it in stride and laughed about it.

Every time one of these things happened, I felt like a million bucks.

Except once.

A television reporter came to the Village Inn to do a story about outdoor dining venues in the city. After someone told them I was working in the kitchen and explained who I was, they thought it was a nice addition to the story and asked to interview me on camera. That moment was very awkward for me. I mean, here they were, featuring me as a guy who recently worked in a movie, but I was now working in a restaurant kitchen handling pickle spears. There's nothing wrong with working in a restaurant, but the moment reminded me of the Kevin Bacon movie, *The Big Picture*.

In that film, Kevin plays a struggling film director who just got out of film school in Los Angeles and is looking to find potential investors for a movie. He eventually talks to a restaurant owner about investing, and the owner says, "Oh, you're a director? You should meet our bus boy, he's a director, too."

Speaking of Kevin Bacon

The 6 Degrees of Kevin Bacon game, if you don't already know, makes connections from the famous actor Kevin Bacon, to any other actor in Hollywood, by connecting movies they have been in with shared co-stars.

For instance, Kevin Bacon can be connected to the comedian Billy Crystal in four degrees:

→ Kevin Bacon was in *Animal House* with John Belushi

→ John Belushi was in *The Blues Brothers* with Dan Aykroyd

→ Dan Aykroyd was in *Dr. Detroit* with Fran Drescher

→ Fran Drescher was in *This is Spinal Tap* with Billy Crystal

You can probably find other, faster ways to connect these two, but that's one example of how to play the game.

Now, because of the famous people that appeared in the first two TMNT films, like Sam Rockwell, Elias Koteas, and David Warner, it's possible to link any TMNT cast member to many other famous actors in this same type of game. For instance, you can connect Mark Caso (Leonardo in TMNT II) to Cher, the heralded singer and actress, in 3 degrees:

→ Mark Caso (Leo) was in *TMNT 2: Secret of the Ooze* with David Warner
→ David Warner was in *Time After Time* with Malcolm McDowell
→ Malcolm McDowell was in *The Player*, with Cher

Here's a secret to the game's success: with a connection to a movie like *The Player*, that featured cameos by literally dozens of famous stars, it's easy to connect with almost any other movie actor ever.

Here's me to Charlie Chaplin in four steps...

→ Kenn Scott was in *TMNT* with Brian Tochi (voice of Leonardo)
→ Brian Tochi was in *The Player* with Scott Glenn
→ Scott Glenn was in *Apocalypse Now* with Marlon Brando
→ Marlon Brando was in *The Countess From Hong Kong* with Charlie Chaplin

Here's my favorite, Kenn Scott to Elvis in two steps:

→ Kenn was in *Star Hunter* with Stella Stevens
→ Stella Stevens was in *Girls, Girls, Girls* with Elvis

By the way...*Star Hunter* is one of the worst movies ever made, and I'm one of the worst actors in it.

This movie is a low budget piece of poop, produced by Stella Stevens' son Andrew Stevens. It's about a group of high school football players and cheerleaders (played by actors all in their late 20's and early 30's) whose bus breaks down in a crappy part of the big city, and they become prey to an evil alien who's hunting for sport. Basically, it's a complete, low-budget rip off of the great action film, *Predator,* but with a shitty script, shitty sets, shitty acting (except the great Roddy McDowall), and a shitty alien with a glowing red penis around its neck. I was fascinated by Stella Stevens and the fact that she had worked with my rock-n-roll idol, Elvis. I asked her what Elvis was like and she said, "He was the stupidest man I ever met and he was drunk all the time." Well...that was somewhat disappointing.

THE THINGS WE DO FOR LUST

One night, after work, I was hanging at the Village Inn having some drinks in the bar with my friend, a waiter named Tony. At one point, this very pretty girl with short, blonde hair approaches me. "I hear you were a Ninja Turtle," she said with a smile of pearly white teeth.

I nodded dumbly and managed to mutter out, "Uh-hunh." She had such great, friendly energy, and she was adorably cute.

She said, "Is it true?"

I nodded. "Yeah, it's true. I'm Kenn. What's your name?"

"I'm Stephanie." We shook hands and she continued. "So, if you were a turtle, you must move pretty good?" My buddy Tony laughed.

I smiled, "Yeah, I move pretty good. What about you?"

She leaned against the bar, "I teach aerobics and I was a cheerleader."

Don't forget, this was right at the end of the '80s and aerobics instructors, not to mention cheerleaders, were all common parts of young men's fantasy discussions at the time. Jane Fonda had launched an aerobics craze in the early '80s, *The Twenty Minute Workout* had been on TV getting men excited, and now exercise classes across the country were packed with fit, leotard-clad women jumping around yelling "Hoo, Hoo!" If you wanted visual motivation to work out, all you had to do was go to the gym, get on a cardio machine, and stare at the class while you labored through your exercise. For young men at the time, it was easy to fall for cute, fit aerobics instructors. And it was happening to me, right there.

For the next little while I asked Stephanie about all things aerobics. She told me she had competed in the mixed-pairs division of the *Reebok National Aerobics Championships*. I didn't know what that was, but I acted interested.

For this competition, participants choreograph three-minute aerobic routines to music and get judged on their appearance and presentation, like a figure skater or a gymnast. I told her how cool I thought that was and it sounded like fun. I was just thrilled that we were connecting. Because of my inexperience with women, I wasn't sure what the next step was, I just knew if I could keep the conversation going, that at least was a good thing.

She told me I should do aerobics competitions because I'd probably be pretty good at it. I laughed and told her it sounded really cool and I'd love to try it sometime. She even said something about how cool it would be if we could be teammates in a competition. Of course, I agreed.

Then her friend came over. "C'mon, Steph. We've gotta go."

Damn! They were leaving. Then something totally cool happened. She said, "Give me your phone number. I'll call you about the competition."

This was before cell phones, so I wrote my mother's home phone number on a napkin and handed it to her. She took the napkin and placed it in her purse, then smiled and pointed her finger at me, "You're not afraid, are you?"

"No, I'm not afraid," I said. We both laughed and said our goodbyes.

About a week later Stephanie called me, and she wasn't playing.

Based on our brief discussion at the bar, she had called her aerobics partner and fired him, saying that she had found somebody else to work with. She had scheduled a choreographer to fly in from Florida the following weekend, so that she and I could work out our routine and get ready for a competition in Atlanta...just a few weeks away.

Holy shit!

I was just trying to hook up with this cute girl in a bar and now I found myself being Shang-hai'd for an aerobics competition? This was crazy, I didn't know the first thing about aerobic routines and contests. What I did know however, was that this girl had fired her partner and made me a part of her plan, apparently based on our brief conversation at a bar. I didn't want to let her down, so I agreed to do it. In reality, I was just committing to a tremendous amount of work to try and get laid.

Over the next several weeks, I joined her at the gym, learned an aerobics routine with jumps and kicks, got a custom-made, skin-tight bodysuit with gold sparkle on it, traveled to Atlanta, and won the gold medal in regional mixed pairs for the *Reebok National Aerobic Championships*...and I wore a dance belt for the first time in my life.

If you don't already know, a dance belt is a man's jockstrap with a thong for the back. Dancers wear them under their skin-tight costumes to hold their penis and testicles in place and not produce unsightly bulges under the costume. The night before the competition, I didn't even know these were a thing and found out I had to have one. Without it, the audience can become obsessed with analyzing your package and lose focus on your overall presentation. To address the issue, another competitor, who was friends with Stephanie, said I could use one of his extra ones. He assured me it had been laundered. I took it hesitantly. Despite the fact that it was clean, I wrapped toilet paper around the thong part that goes up your butt before putting it on.

Despite spending so much time together, Stephanie and I never fooled around the entire time we trained. It just never seemed

143

appropriate to cross that line once we were teammates. However, the night we won the competition, we went to a pizza place across the street from our hotel to celebrate and drink beer, something I'm very good at.

We both got a little tipsy and then made our way back to the hotel. At that point, she giggled and said, "Can I ask you something?"

"Of course," I said.

She smiled and giggled some more, "How come you've never tried to kiss me?"

So, I did.

This was the moment we had both been waiting for! We made our way back to my room and started fooling around. We kissed and it got hot. We pulled each other's clothes off. We were getting really passionate.

Then she vomited beer and pizza all over the hotel room.

BABY'S FIRST CAST & CREW

If you work on a Hollywood movie, there are a couple of different ways you might be able to see it in a theater before it comes out to the public.

The coolest way is to go to a red-carpet premiere with celebrities and the press and photo ops and all that stuff. Not everybody who works on a movie crew gets invited to these, but the main actors, the various producers, and the director go.

Another way to see a movie before it comes out to the public is when the producers organize a "cast & crew screening." At a cast & crew screening, everybody who worked on the film is invited. It's usually the first time many of these people have seen each other in several months, sometimes up to a year. Because of the deep bonds that were formed on the set, this is a time for everybody to reconnect and catch up with each other's lives. Then, the lights go down and they watch the movie, cheering, laughing, and enjoying the film to its fullest, recalling and whispering about moments on the set when certain scenes were being shot.

It's cool because, as a collective group of moviemakers, you're now seeing what all the work everybody did looks like on screen. There are no more ladders and sound stages or PA's running around with walkie-talkies; it's now just all the quiet, subtle stuff that took place between "action" and "cut." The camera sees things in a way we can't when we are just standing on the set watching.

145

The close-up on an actor's face, the realism of special FX make-up, or the unique camera angle, all look totally different on a 50-foot screen than you might have guessed as the filming took place.

Luckily, I was invited to attend one of these cast and crew screenings for the first TMNT movie. I was still in North Carolina waiting to see if they were going to make a second movie, and the screening was in New York. They had one in Los Angeles, too, but there were so many people who worked on the film from New York, including several executives, that they organized one there, as well. They sent me an invitation because I was on the cast & crew list as "Stunts-Raphael" and "Talkative Foot #2." I had to get my own plane ticket and get myself a hotel room, but nothing was going to keep me away from that screening.

I got a call from Ric Meyers, a writer in New York who worked with *Inside Kung-Fu,* a martial arts magazine I had been reading since I was a kid. Ric would also be at the screening as a member of the press and wanted to do an article about the martial arts used in the film. Since I was the only martial arts performer that would be in New York for the screening, the production company had given him my number and he was eager to meet and talk to get the inside story.

When I got to New York and made my way to the theater, I didn't really know too many people because many of them were office workers for the Henson group or the distribution company New Line Cinema. I'm sure there were others, but I did not recognize them at the time. Micha (Michelangelo) lived in New York and was there, he welcomed me with open arms.

I handed my invitation to the woman in the box office and went inside, sitting by myself. When the lights went dark, it was a crazy experience. I was on pins and needles, waiting to see myself in a real Hollywood movie and watch my dreams come to life. At the same time, I was by myself with no real friends or family to share it with. It was super exciting, but also a little lonely. I wasn't depressed about it, but I felt very isolated.

As I stared up at the screen, I could not watch the movie like a regular audience member and lose myself in the story. I was caught up remembering all the behind-the-scenes moments and anticipating all the action scenes that we had done. It was hard to pay attention to story details when I was thinking things like, "Wow, that's what April's apartment looks like on film," or, "I remember the day we shot that, it was raining outside."

Selfishly anticipating my appearances on screen, I didn't have to wait long. About fifteen minutes in, Raphael, angry about losing his sai, goes to the movies by himself to chill out. It's on this trip that he first encounters Casey Jones and rolls over the taxi while chasing him. When the scene started, I slid to the edge of my seat. I was not there the night they shot the scene with the baseball and cricket bats. This was the first time I was seeing the scene in which Nam got dropped into the trashcan on his head and broke his nose. It happened in the footage that's still actually in the film. I felt empathetic pain as my friend crashed down. I was also like, "Damn, that's what got me this job!"

After that, Raph chases Casey across the street and hits the cab. When I saw myself roll over the cab hood, that's when I thought, "Well, that was pretty cool, but it seemed so much bigger in real life."

Outside of seeing myself in the background of one shot of *Dracula's Widow* on VHS tape for a split second, this was really the first time I was seeing a performance of mine, in a movie, actually playing on a screen. It was an electrifying thrill. Unfortunately, it was over in the blink of an eye and the movie kept on playing. I spent the next few minutes thinking about what I had just seen, judging my performance, and salivating even more to see my next appearance.

Not long after that, April O'Neil finds herself facing menacing Foot Soldiers in the subway. My eyes opened wide as I watched Raphael come bounding down the platform and quickly dispatch the Foot with a double jumping front kick, a tornado kick, and some punches and elbows. Again, being my own worst critic, I was disappointed that my jumping kicks looked as low as they did. I also noticed that they never even used the shot of me coming out of the tunnel when I thought I was going to be crushed by a subway. Regardless, it still looked cool as hell and it was the first visible Ninja Turtle fight against bad guys ever shown on film. Before that, it was just a brush with Casey Jones, and the four turtles beating up some thieves in the beginning, of which you could only hear sound effects.

After that scene, I was in for a long wait until my next appearance as a Foot or a Turtle, so I settled in to watch the movie. It was during the filming of all these interstitial dramatic scenes that the Foot Soldiers and I were practicing fights, playing cards, or working out, so this was the first time I was seeing any of this stuff at all.

Eventually, we got to the scene in which Raphael argues with Leonardo and then leaves the apartment to head up to the roof to be alone. From then on, it's a combination of me and Nam doubling Raphael, and me being a Foot Soldier.

Once Raphael crashes through the skylight and falls to the floor, it kicks off the biggest choreography of the film with all the Foot crashing into the apartment and fighting all the remaining turtles, including the "fellow 'chucker" scene. I was disappointed to see that they had cut the Talkative Foot #2 "turtle soup" moment, but my disappointment was abated when I heard my own voice shout, "Bisentos, now!" just a minute later. I was so excited to hear my own voice, it's hard to put into words what that meant as a milestone in my journey. This was my first job out of college and I could now say I had uttered dialogue in a real martial arts action movie. That was huge!

From that moment forward, seeing all the various parts of the film in which I had participated gave me nothing but joy. I saw all the locations we had filmed and remembered all the excitement of shooting. I sat in the dark, entranced in the moment, never wanting it to end.

But, it did...and the audience cheered.

Watching it that first time was an exciting blur of story, colors, puppet suits, and fighting. I did think the movie was kind of visually dark, with an artsy, low-budget feel to it. In that sense, it reminded me of the original *Highlander,* which is one of my favorite movies of all time. *Highlander,* like TMNT, feels more like an art school film than a big Hollywood action blockbuster. In retrospect, I think Steve Barron may have been using shadow and darkness to mask a certain cartoony-ness that might otherwise have come out. But, that's just my guess.

Because it's a cast & crew screening, everybody sat patiently through the credits looking for their names and their friends' names and applauding appropriately. The first names to go by in the credits for this film were a thank you to Renay and Mark Freedman, the couple that was responsible for handling all the licensing rights for the turtles. The second set of names that come up are the four actor turtles, Josh, Michelan, Leif, and David. After that, there's a few key crew credits, and then the full cast list. You can only imagine how thrilled I was when the 26th name down, in a list of only 30 credits, was "Talkative Foot #2–Kenn Troum." Then, after more crew credits roll by, the stunt credits appeared. And there again, under "Turtle Stunt Doubles," along with all the guys from Hong Kong, and Ernie Reyes, Jr., it says "Kenn Troum." Two credits in my first movie; kickass!

The lights came up and people turned eagerly to chat with their friends about what they had just seen. I stayed for a few minutes, drinking in the energy, then headed outside to meet Ric Meyers for our scheduled interview. We went to a nearby diner to talk further.

It was during that interview that I was to discover that Ric was a prolific writer of books and for magazines. Much to my surprise and sheer delight, I learned that Ric was also "Wade Barker" the ghost author of my favorite *Ninja Master* adventure books from when I was a kid. He was the man responsible for *Million Dollar Massacre* and the line "The hitman's guts started pouring out from the hole between his legs." This day was turning out to be more incredible every moment. Ric and I spent a good amount of time together while he asked me all about Pat Johnson, the guys from Hong Kong, and my experiences working on the film.

After the interview, I returned to my hotel to pick up my stuff and make it back to the airport. Time to get back to my reality in the restaurant kitchen.

ONLY PUBLIC APPEARANCE

A few weeks later, before the movie actually came out to the public, the producers decided to try a promotional stunt. It would turn out to be the only time ever, that any of the turtle costumes from the original movie made a live public appearance.

The producers wanted the turtles to appear on the field at a halftime show of a high school football game in Phoenix, Arizona and do some martial arts. They wanted to test out the process and gauge the cost to see if it was worth it to book more appearances around the country. All the other stunt turtles lived in Hong Kong and it was too expensive to fly them over, so the producers got Ernie Reyes, Jr. and me to do it. They flew us to Arizona and sent a couple of people to help us get in and out of the suits.

We got dressed in the football fieldhouse, which doubled as the school's wrestling room. One of the 8x10 photos that I sign today at comic cons comes from my own personal camera and was taken in that room. I posed on the wrestling mat and Ernie took the picture for me.

We stepped through a couple of choreographed moves to get ready and eventually we were announced onto the field. As we walked out, we were talking to each other through the heads, "Let's go over here." "Okay, let's start. Throw a punch," etc. We did fight choreography and we danced with the cheerleaders.

I worked my ass off, trying hard to represent a good character. I believed in what I was doing and wanted this movie to be successful. I had dressed up as my high school mascot, the Greensboro Grimsley Whirlie, for football games, so I knew you had to go all out to create a fun, likable character. I did that for this crowd, jumping up and down with the cheerleaders and dancing to the marching band. It was hot as hell, but besides sweating my ass off again, it was fun to do.

Fortunately, we were only outside for 10 minutes or so before they had to start the game again, so the whole thing was short and sweet...plus we made SAG money for the day. Things all seemed to be going pretty well.

PRIVATE SCREENING

A few weeks later, in March, excitement was building for the release of the movie. Television commercials were running and people were talking about it. My friends were all calling to congratulate me.

Back then, as is the case today, most new movies opened in theaters on Fridays, which meant the theaters received the actual copy of the film at least a day or so before.

I convinced the manager of a local theater in Greensboro to show the film on Thursday night at midnight for my family and friends. He agreed because he couldn't get in trouble for that since it would technically be Friday, opening day.

Before the midnight screening, we threw a party at my mom's house and all my friends and family got dressed up like a Hollywood premiere, then we headed to the theater.

As the movie played, I shouted to my friends and pointed out all the parts that I was in.

On the way home, my friend Tony and I rode with a co-worker from the Village Inn named Lisa. Lisa was a tough North Carolina girl. I had the hots for her and we spent some quality time together while working at the restaurant. Lisa also had an ex-boyfriend who was a full-on redneck. That night, after the movie, Tony actually drove us home in Lisa's car because she had been drinking.

Unfortunately, it turns out her ex-boyfriend was out at that late hour and recognized her car as we drove down the road. He decided he didn't like seeing "his girl" in a car with other dudes, so *(start reading with a Southern accent here)*...he commenced to a followin' us pretty darn close in his vickle with his buddies. When we done got to Tony's house, redneck boyfriend and his pals took to confrontin' us right up thar in Tony's driveway, gettin' all ornery. Tony was tryin' to talk to 'em all real peaceable-like, but he looked pretty ridikulus in his blazer and bow tie. They was hankerin' for a fight, that is until Tony's roommate done come out tha house with a deer rifle clutched in his paws and fired a warnin' shot over thar heads. That set 'em back a pace, so they hopped in their vickle and tore out *(end Southern accent here)*.

Only thing is, when those boneheads drove off they got their stupid car stuck in a ditch at the bottom of Tony's front yard. They actually had to come back to the house a few minutes later and ask to call a tow truck. Idiots.

And I went home with the girl.

WORLD PREMIERE

The first Teenage Mutant Ninja Turtles movie was released into the world in March of 1990. It was five years after the turtles were originally created by Kevin Eastman and Peter Laird in comic book form, and just a year or so since the television cartoon was released. At the time, people were tearing down the Berlin Wall and the very first web server was created. The radio was filled with pop hits from Madonna, Phil Collins, Janet Jackson, and New Kids on the Block and movie theaters were showing *Ghost*, *Home Alone*, and *Pretty Woman*.

Teenage Mutant Ninja Turtles was dismissed by many critics as trash. However, the famous movie critic Roger Ebert did give it 2.5 out of 3 stars. Regardless of what critics said, it appealed to fans everywhere. During its run, the film would make 160 million dollars in America, becoming the most successful "independent" film of all time; that is, until *My Big Fat Greek Wedding* came out a few years later and almost doubled it.

Just so you know, an "independent film" is any movie that is produced by anybody other than a major movie studio. In the old days, the major studios included Warner Bros., Paramount, 20th Century Fox, Metro-Goldwyn-Mayer, Columbia, RKO, and Disney. If any other person or group put together money and made a film without money from those studios, they were considered "independent" films. These could be tiny, low-budget, exploitation movies like the ones that Phil Smoot and Earl Owesnby were making in North Carolina, or they could be larger productions with famous movie stars produced by independent guys with a lot of cash. TMNT was put together by Golden Harvest from Hong Kong and New Line Cinema from the U.S., both small players compared to the studios, thus, making it an independent film.

Turtle fever inspired a period of great prosperity in strip mall Tae Kwon Do schools and pizza places. There were even public warnings to stop kids from going down into the sewers looking for the turtles.

Together with other turtle merchandise and licensing, the franchise would go on to spread across the world, influencing culture and business, and grossing billions of dollars in licensed sales over the following 10 years. It continues to this day to be a billion-dollar property with new movies, toys, and TV shows continually being produced.

In 1990, though, it was still a basically unknown property when the movie came out and I was still living at my mom's place in Greensboro wondering if the film would be successful enough to warrant a sequel.

THE FIRST PAT JOHNSON CALL

After the premiere, the movie was doing well at the box office, and I was reveling in the joy of it all, answering questions and having fun stories to tell to friends and family. But, I was also going about the mundane business of working at the restaurant.

Then I got a call from Pat Johnson.

"Hello, may I speak with Kenn please." I recognized Pat's distinctive voice right away.

Pat said, "As you know, the movie opened very well, and we just got word that they are going to do a sequel. They called me and want me to start putting the action team in place."

My heart was beating faster and faster.

Pat continued, "We won't be bringing in any guys from Hong Kong like last time, that was too expensive, and we have some great talent here. So, I'd like you to do the action for Raphael again."

It was jaw-dropping for me to hear those words.

"Pat," I stammered out, "thank you so much. I can't tell you how much I appreciate it."

Despite the good fortune that just came my way, I decided to take a chance and see if I could make it even better...

"Pat, you know, if there's any chance to be an actor turtle...you know, in case there's like an opening or something for any of the characters, like I said in my letter before, my ultimate goal is to be an actor, and I think maybe...

157

Pat cut me off, "Let's start with this, son, and see what happens. Be happy you got a job. I think you're off to a good start."

Pat was right. He knew my goals and was helping me in every way he could. "Just be patient," he said, "You've got a long life ahead of you. I'll call you soon and let you know what's next."

He hung up the phone and I started jumping up and down in the kitchen shouting "Yes! Yes! Hell Yes!"

INSIDE KUNG-FU TROUBLE

I quit my job at the Village Inn and decided I would just wait out the next month or so until the movie started. I told my friend Steve, as well as Tony and a couple of guys from the restaurant who wanted to move to L.A. with us, that I had to stay in North Carolina and work on the film for a few months. They all agreed that it would be a good thing for them to go ahead and move without me, and I could catch up with them in California after the second movie wrapped in the fall. They would find us a place to live and scout out the territory. It was all working out pretty well.

Then I suffered another stumble.

Inside Kung-fu Magazine came out. The cover was a picture of Donatello and it said, "Teenage Mutant Kung-fu Turtles?" and it was based on Ric Meyers' interview with me. When I saw it on the newsstand, I was excited and bought multiple copies to send to my family.

I quickly shuffled through the magazine to find the article. It was several pages, filled with my story and anecdotes from working on the film. It even had personal photographs of mine that I had shared with them, including one of me in the turtle costume with the head off standing next to Pat Johnson.

I couldn't wait to show everybody. I even put a copy of the magazine in the mail and sent it to Pat Johnson with a note thanking him for all that he had done for me.

A couple of days later, I called Pat to see how he liked it.

He didn't.

"Kenn, I'm a little upset," he said.

Oh, shit, I thought. "Why Pat, what happened?"

Pat proceeded to explain to me two things I had done wrong without knowing it. First, in the article, I had mentioned Brandy Yuen, the "Martial Arts Consultant" from Hong Kong who worked with Pat during the film and assisted him by translating the choreography to the Asian stunt guys. The article had given Brandy too much credit for his contribution. Pat told me this was disrespectful to him and undermined his position and reputation as the stunt coordinator/fight choreographer on the film.

I was mortified. The very last thing I ever intended to do was disrespect Pat. He had been like a father to me and helped me every step of the way. I thought I had done good by telling what I had seen and experienced on the film. I certainly recognized Pat for all the great work he had done, I didn't realize anything I said was harmful to that.

In the long run, it wasn't the end of the world. Pat wasn't really happy about it, however, he wasn't going to hold onto it. He just told me to be more careful in the future. Then he told me about the second thing I had done wrong.

David Chan, the producer from Golden Harvest, had called Pat and was very upset that I had supplied the magazine with the picture of me in costume, holding the turtle head in my hands. The producers didn't want any pictures of incomplete turtle costumes in the public eye, they felt it would undermine the integrity of the characters. Now, I had just published one in a national magazine. David actually called me personally to tell me how upset he was, but there was nothing that could be done.

When all was said and done, there wasn't really that much damage or fallout from it, so they let it slide. But, I didn't do myself any favors with that article.

160

It does not feel good to have the people who hire you upset at something you did. I don't like fucking up, but either through naiveté or stupidity, I have done it many times in my life. I think we all probably do it as some point. Unfortunately, I did it on my first movie...to Pat Johnson. And when Pat Johnson's upset with you, it feels like you let down Santa Claus.

THE SECOND PAT JOHNSON CALL

A couple of weeks went by and the furor over the magazine article had died down. Nobody thought I was trying to be a jerk, it was just the mistake of a rookie, so they let it go. It was then that I got another call from Pat Johnson. Again, I recognized his voice right away.

"Hi, Pat," I said.

"Kenn, I just want you to know that Josh Pais the actor is not coming back to play Raphael. The producer, David Chan, is going to be looking for someone to replace him. Thought you might like to know...but you didn't hear it from me." Then he hung up.

I stared at the phone for a second. Pat had just presented me with an opportunity.

I quickly found a call sheet I had taken from the first movie. It had every crew member's name and contact info on it. I got the phone number for David Chan off the back. I dialed with trembling fingers and, after a few tension-filled rings, David answered, "Hello."

"Hi David, this is Kenn Troum."

He responded, "Yes, Kenn, hello."

I plowed forward, "I just want you to know that I am looking forward to working with Pat Johnson on the stunt team, but I also want you to know that my goal is to be an actor, so if there are any opportunities to do that on this next film, and move into one of the actor turtle roles, I think I could do a great job. Just wanted you to know that."

The line was silent, it felt like an eternity.

Then he said. "Well, Kenn, we are looking for a new Raphael, but we already want to use you for the stunts and fighting."

I kept moving forward. "Yes, I know, and I'm very excited about that. But, my ultimate goal is to be an actor and I saw what the guys did last year, and I think I could do that."

David cleared his throat. "Ok, Kenn. Here's what you do...Make a video of you doing scenes from the first movie and acting like Raphael. Talk like him, move like him, then send it to me. Has to be on my desk Tuesday morning, that's when we are talking about it, understand?"

Of course I understood. I understood that I just got myself a chance to audition for the main part of Raphael!

I thanked David and went into overdrive. It was already Friday evening on the east coast. I needed to find a video camera, pick out scenes, get somebody to film it the next day, and get it sent overnight delivery to Los Angeles.

The next morning I borrowed a video camera from my friend. I got my buddy Tony from the Village Inn to shoot video of me standing in my mom's front yard. I wore a green T-shirt and stomped around the yard saying lines like, "Yeah, Leo, I figured I'd redecorate, you know...a couple of throw pillows, a TV news reporter."

Everything was closed on Sunday, so the plan was to overnight the videotape on Monday to arrive at David's office by the Tuesday morning deadline.

Monday rolled around and I opened the phone book to find the local FedEx or some other overnight delivery service.

Then I realized it was Memorial Day.

Everything was closed.

163

In all my excitement, I had totally overlooked the holiday weekend. I started to panic. I tore through the yellow pages for other delivery options, desperate to find a solution. They were all closed. I considered flying to L.A. and delivering it myself, so I called the airlines to price tickets. I called Delta Airlines and it turns out airlines actually had delivery services that I didn't know about. They told me that if I brought my package to the airport, they could fly it to Los Angeles and deliver it to the final address overnight no problem...for $150. Holy shit, that's a lot of money, but considering the circumstances, it was a quick decision. I already had the job as the stunt turtle, so I knew I could afford the gamble. I drove to the airport and sent it off.

It was agony waiting the next 24 hours. I imagine it's kind of like what contestants on shows like *America's Got Talent* feel when they are waiting to find out if they move on to the next round of becoming a superstar, or if their dreams are dashed upon the rocks. On Tuesday afternoon, I called David to make sure he got the tape.

"Yes, thank you, Kenn. I received it. It is very good," he said. "We have about 40 other people we're going to look at here in Los Angeles, so I will let you know what happens. Thanks for sending it." Then he hung up.

Well, fuck.

I didn't know I was going to be up against so many, most-likely amazingly talented and well-qualified guys, who actually live in L.A. and probably have agents and cool stuff like that.

I consoled myself, knowing that, no matter what, I was still going to be on the action team and earn a weekly SAG contract. That's pretty cool, pretty good money, and would help set me up for my move to Los Angeles.

Then, a few days later I got a call, "Hello Kenn, it's David Chan."

"Hi, David. Nice to hear from you," I said.

"I wanted to call to congratulate you," he said, "You are the new Raphael!"

My heart leaped. He explained that they felt I was a good fit for the role and they would be hiring somebody else to double Raph in the stunt work. They felt that my martial arts background and my familiarity with the suits would make me an asset to the first unit and they could replace me with another stunt guy on the second unit. This was amazing! Another step closer to action-herohood.

Just a few months before, I had been staring at the actor turtles on the first movie, envious of their position, wanting to be them.

Now, I was one of them!

Secret Agent, Man!

I n order to get me to costume fittings and start preparing for the role, a contract needed to be negotiated. David Chan told me that the new unit production manager for the film, Terry Morse, was going to reach out in the next few days and finalize my contract.

A Unit Production Manager or UPM is basically the guy or girl that's in charge of the actual "manufacturing" of a movie. They hire and fire all the crew members, handle all the contracts, manage the bank account, and spend every day on the set, making sure that everything is moving forward and costs are being controlled. They're in charge of getting the movie made and trying to get everyone to work as cheaply as possible to do it.

I had no agent and I certainly didn't know how contract negotiations worked. I needed to prepare for the discussion with the producer, so I opened the yellow pages and called a local talent agency in Greensboro. It was called Marilyn's Agency and they mostly handled people who did print ads for local newspapers, magazines, local TV commercials, that kind of stuff. It was owned by a woman named, get this, Marilyn. I told her my story and asked if she could handle the discussion with the producer for me. Marilyn honorably protested that she didn't feel right handling a simple phone call and taking 10% of my income; it wasn't that complicated and I could handle it myself. She asked what I made on the first film as a turtle, I told her SAG minimum, around $1,500 per week. Marilyn told me to up it to $2,000 and that would be a reasonable deal they would probably agree to. If I had any problems after that, she said I could call her.

When I got the call from the producer, Terry Morse, I was super nervous. My palms were sweating. He told me that we needed to put a contract in place that would cover the three weeks of rehearsal and then nine weeks of shooting. He offered me $1,500 per week for all of it.

I mustered up some balls and told him that I thought it would be fair for me to make $2,000 per week since I had worked on the first film.

He hemmed and hawed for a second but agreed pretty quickly. I was probably making less than Micha and Leif, who had agents negotiating for them, so I was most likely a bargain. Terry then tried to negotiate me down to $1,500 for the first three weeks of rehearsal, as if they were less important.

I remembered things Marilyn told me and stuck to my guns.

"No," I said, "I think it's fair to keep the rate the same throughout." He agreed without much pushback. Then we hung up.

I'm sure I was a cheap deal, but I had just negotiated my first Hollywood contract. I felt like I was kicking ass.

GO FURTHER EAST, YOUNG MAN

The first order of business was flying to London to visit the Henson Creature Shop and get my personal, custom-fitted Raphael suit made. The only hitch was, I didn't have a passport.

I'd never been anywhere out of the country in my life, except Tijuana, Mexico, and back then, you didn't need a passport to go across those borders, just a driver's license. Ordinarily it can take several weeks or even months to get a passport, but...if you have emergency circumstances, you can go, in person, to certain offices in major cities and get a passport in one day.

The producers made arrangements for me to leave Greensboro at 5:30 A.M. and fly to Washington D.C. Once there, I was to go to the federal passport office, submit my application, and wait to get a passport by the end of the business day. Then, I had to get back to the airport and be on a plane to London by 8 P.M. It was a logistical challenge in which any one little hitch could screw it up. I felt like I was being challenged with a mission to accomplish, kind of like some Joseph Campbell hero's journey stuff.

Despite my grand illusions of a heroic journey, it was a pretty mundane and boring process; just a lot of traveling and waiting.

After I turned in my application, I had to wait all day for the processing. I had a suitcase with me, so it wasn't like I could bounce around D.C. whiling away the time sightseeing, plus I was super tired from getting up so early. So, while I was waiting, I caught a taxi to a nearby shopping mall, bought a ticket to the movies, and with my suitcase next to me, I settled into a theater to watch a matinee of *Back to the Future III*. It wasn't long before I fell asleep, woken only when the movie ended and they came to clean the theater.

I made my way back to the passport office. Luckily, I got a passport with no issues, then caught a cab and made my way to the airport for the long flight to London.

LONDON CALLING

I landed in Heathrow Airport in London early the next morning. When I came off the plane, there was a guy waiting for me with my name printed out on a sign. I'd never had that happen before. We walked to the parking lot and found his car. He proceeded to drive down the wrong side of the road and we made our way through London, all the way to the Henson Creature Shop where they were just starting their work day. For me, it was going on 24 hours since I had started the journey. I was tired, but excited.

The Henson shop was an unremarkable brick building sitting on an unremarkable street corner; no signs, bright lights, or anything to draw attention to it. I walked up to the front door and rang the bell.

A voice called from the intercom: "Yes, Hallo?"

I leaned forward to the speaker, "Yes, it's Kenn Troum."

The door buzzed open and I entered what I knew would be a mystical world of colorful Muppets and other fantastic creations.

I was wrong.

To my dismay, the interior was no different than the exterior, dark and drab. It was a dusty warehouse space filled with work tables, buckets of paint, scraps of wood, and piles of fabric.

What was super awesome, however, was a series of clay statues that occupied the main area of the workshop. Artists were perched on ladders, using tiny metal carving tools to shape life-size clay versions of Tokka and Rahzar, the giant snapping turtle and

wolverine in the story. Although I did not know who those char-
acters were at the time, it was incredible to see them in full size.
The clay sculptures were the first steps for creating the costumes.
It was the same process that I was there to undertake for the
Raphael costume.

BESPOKE TAILORING

Getting a custom costume made starts with getting a mold of the performer's body.

When they made the cast of my body, I had to put on one of the skintight lycra bodysuits I wore under the costume in the first movie. In those things, just like in my aerobics outfit, you can see every basic curve and detail of a person's body...every curve and detail.

I was led, in this skintight onesie, down into the basement of the workshop, where I was greeted by five guys with heavy Cockney accents. They seemed more like soccer hooligans than guys that made cute Muppets. They all wore white painter suits and looked like a crew of English Oompa-Loompas. Their job was to make a mold of my body using hot, wet plaster of paris bandages, and then let it all harden into a shell.

The first thing they did was tie cloth loops around my wrists and then suspend my arms out to the sides using cords hanging from the ceiling. I looked like a capital "T." Apparently, this was the exact same spot where David Bowie stood to get his body cast made for *Labyrinth*. They filled buckets with hot water and dipped the dry plaster bandages into the water, then they started applying them to my body.

It doesn't matter who you are, or who's doing it, but if someone puts warm plaster of paris on your whole body, and especially around your crotch, if you're 21 years of age, and in good shape,

172

with good circulation, that bit of warm, wet stimulation is gonna get some blood flowing in that area. Heck, it's only natural. At least it was for me. Having several people gently apply warm, moist pressure to my nether region resulted in a biological reaction commonly known as *dickus erectus*.

One of the Cockney guys was down on his knees, gently pressing the hot, moist bandages around my crotch, and he smiled and said, "Gettin' a little excited are you," laughing and indicating to the others the growing bulge constrained under the bandages and lycra.

I smiled, "Can't help it, you're just so good looking," I said. Fortunately, that got a laugh out of them.

Once they finished applying the plaster, they attached wooden beams to the whole contraption to help keep its shape. I had to stand still and wait about 20 minutes before it hardened. The plaster that is.

Once it was dry, they used crowbars to separate the mold into two parts, the front and back. Later, they could put the two halves back together and inject the now empty mold with liquid fiberglass. That would create a perfect fiberglass replica of my body. On top of a fiberglass replica like this, they would pile on clay and sculpt the character of Raphael. Once they took a mold of the finished Raphael clay sculpture, they could suspend my fiberglass body in the center of that new Raphael mold, inject the mold with foam latex, and that would form a perfect turtle-shaped costume around my physique. Once that all dried, they would remove my fiberglass body from inside the foam turtle body and have an empty turtle costume ready to wear. Then they would just need to paint it.

They would have done all of this for me, but because they had already done this process a year before with Josh and Nam, they already had a sculpture of Raphael ready to go. They simply needed to put my fiberglass body into the mold of that original Raphael, and voila, they would have an original Raphael suit, custom fitted to me.

Eventually they determined everything was okay with the body cast and they sent me to the hotel for the night. That was fine by me because I was exhausted; I'd been up for over 30 hours. If I had been more of a confident traveler at that time, I probably would have explored London a little bit, but I was dead tired and intent on staying in and keeping a low profile. I was also being diligent about working out hard to make the most of my martial arts action-hero opportunity, so I wasn't drinking or partying. So, rather than step out of my hotel and explore this strange new land, I stayed in, ordered a tuna fish sandwich, and watched *Dr. Who* for the first time.

The next day at the workshop, they needed to make a cast of my head and face. They were making a fiberglass helmet for me, on which the entire turtle head and electronic servos would be mounted. The helmet was more than just a covering on my head, it was like a mask that came down around the eyes and across the nose, like the thing Captain America wears, but hard. The helmet had to conform perfectly to each performer's head and face so the weight of the electric motors could sit as comfortably balanced and firm as possible. This inner helmet is the thing that smashed down and broke Nam's nose in the first film.

To make my facial cast, they didn't use plaster of paris, they actually used a wet clay made out of algae. Instead of being hot like the plaster, it was cool to the touch. I put a rubber swimming cap on my head and they applied the cold, wet clay all around my head and face. They stuck two short soda straws through the clay and into my nostrils to make sure I could breathe. Once my head and face were fully encased, I looked like a giant egghead. I had to remain perfectly still for 15 or 20 minutes for it to dry. A lot of people see pictures I have of this process and tell me that it might freak them out to be closed up like that. I focused on deep martial arts, meditative breathing and found the experience really peaceful, kind of like suspended animation. I am not claustrophobic (although one of the other Raphaels was) so I had no problems. Also, when they pull the clay off of your face, it takes all the impurities and dirt that was lodged in your pores with it, so it's like a super high-end facial treatment.

I got a turtle facial.

MEET THE DIRECTOR

I was scheduled to fly out of London's Heathrow airport and back to North Carolina right after the headcast was completed. However, the director of TMNT 2, Michael Pressman, expressed a desire to meet me so that he could feel comfortable with all the actors he was going to be working with. The producers rescheduled my return flight so that I would travel all the way from England to California, spend a night there, meet the director, and return to North Carolina the next day. Talk about some serious jet lag. Fortunately, I didn't care. I was racking up the frequent flyer miles and feeling like a movie star. I also got to fly on Virgin Air. At the time, Virgin Air was one of the nicest airlines you could fly, with great service and nice planes with all the amenities.

Going to L.A., I was nervous about meeting the director. He has the power to veto me and start the process over with somebody else if he wants...or at least that's what I thought to myself.

When I landed, I was picked up at the airport and driven to an office. Not being very familiar with L.A., I had no idea where they took me. I was escorted into an office and presented to Michael. He was a short man with a crown of graying hair. He didn't look like a guy that would direct action movies, he looked like a guy who would teach Sunday school. Regardless, I was intimidated. On the other hand, I was also confident that I was pursuing my calling, or as Joseph Campbell says, "finding my bliss," so I figured my destiny was undeniable.

Michael was very friendly and said hello.

"Kenn," he said, "I just wanted to get together with you. I was told you were a stunt guy, and you did some great work on the first movie, but now you're an actor. It's very important for me, as the director, to feel comfortable that you can handle the dramatic requirements. So, I just wanted to meet you and talk a little bit."

"Great," I said. I was all smiles because I felt that I had everything he might ask for.

Michael asked me some questions about my life and my background in acting and school. We talked about my acting pursuits in high school and college. I told him about the theater awards I had won. We even talked a little bit about the character of Raph and his dynamic with the other turtles. It was a very pleasant conversation, despite the fact that I was feeling judged every minute. We were probably together for about 20 or 30 minutes before Michael brought the conversation to an end.

"Well, Kenn," he said, "I think everything is going to be fine. It was very nice to meet you." We shook hands and I was escorted back down to a waiting car.

I crashed out in the hotel, then flew back to North Carolina the next day. I also got a call from the line producer Terry Morse. My anxiety rose at first because I thought he must be calling to tell me the director had changed his mind.

Instead, he said, "Kenn, everything is good for your body cast. In about a week, you will fly back to London to try on the costume and work with the other guys."

I was barely back home and already another trip to London was scheduled.

I felt like an international, jet-setting, movie star.

LONDON PART II

Flights were a lot easier the second time since I didn't have to get rerouted all over the place to get a passport. My attitude on this second trip to London was similar to the first; keep my head down, do push-ups, order room service, and watch Dr. Who. I wasn't being adventurous in England, but things were going well and I didn't want to mess with the formula.

I flew into Heathrow again and was taken straight to the Henson workshop, again. This time there were a lot more workers all over the place. The nearly completed and painted costumes for Tokka and Rahzar were standing up, supported by fiberglass bodies inside. They were seven feet tall and totally scary looking. A couple of people were methodically stitching hairs into the Rahzar costume one at a time.

The rest of the work area was divided into four quadrants, each quadrant dedicated to one turtle. The fiberglass body of each actor was being used to support various parts of their unique turtle costume. Because I was Raphael, they used red fiberglass to make my body cast. They used purple to make Leif's, orange for Micha's, and blue for Mark's. I darted immediately to the red mannequin and saw my own body cast for the first time, including a perfect recreation of my face from the algae-based mold. Because the eyes were closed, it looked like a dead, plastic version of me; a little creepy, but pretty cool. I also couldn't help but notice the bulge in the crotch. And I was not the only one.

A lot of people at the shop had noticed a large bulge in the red one's crotch. Now, I'm not claiming that I am well-endowed at all, but with all that was going on when they made my body cast, it certainly appears that way in the final statue...although I'm not denying it either. I am happy to report that, behind the scenes, all the crew in the creature shop considered Raphael the turtle with the biggest package. True story.

Once I got over the wonder and awe of all that I saw, they asked me to try on various parts of the turtle costume, as well as the fiberglass helmet that goes under the head. Because I had done it so many times on the first film, I was used to the routine of putting on the lycra suit, covering myself in baby powder and squeezing into the costume bits. This time, the difference was, the parts were literally made for me. No longer was I the "Franken-turtle" of the first movie, made up of different parts of other turtles. I was a pure and complete being all on my own.

I tried on the helmet they made from my face cast. They made a few adjustments by sanding a bit here and cutting a piece off there, but eventually it fit great. Everything seemed to work out well and they determined things were moving in the right direction. They would have more pieces to try as the next couple of days went on, including the complete animatronic head. In the meantime, I could go back to the hotel and relax.

TURTLES REALLY DO EAT PIZZA

When I got to my hotel, I had a message waiting from Micha. All the turtles were there and had cycled through the creature shop earlier in the day. That night, Micha wanted all the actor turtles to meet in the lobby and go have dinner together. It would be the first time that all of us were in the same place at the same time. I was ecstatic to be part of this small, but noteworthy group of short people, and headed down to the lobby.

When we all met, it was Leif Tilden (Donatello), Michelan Sisti (Michelangelo), Mark Caso (Leonardo), and me (Raphael).

Leif was the same old Leif, the mischievous jester. I still really wanted Leif to like me. He seemed so interesting and fun.

Micha was ever smiling and congenial, a true gentleman. He was already playing host to the rest of us and showing leadership by bringing us together on the first night; leadership that he would show throughout the production.

Mark was an unknown commodity to all of us, but he was a super gentle spirit. He was short like the rest of us, under five foot seven, had long hair like a '70s rock star, and exuded a very peaceful nature, kind of like a yoga instructor. When he was younger, Mark was an outstanding gymnastics recruit for UCLA, but at the end of an incredibly grueling practice, he attempted a challenging tumbling routine and wrecked, breaking his neck. He ended up wearing a metal halo device screwed into his skull for several months, his lifestyle severely limited and his athletic career cut short. But, never giving up, Mark fought through rehab, rebuilt his strength and his spirit, and reclaimed his life. Remarkably, he went on to compete at the highest level in USA Championship gymnastics, eventually pursuing an acting career, and ending up as a freakin' Ninja Turtle just a few years later.

That's a story worth its own movie.

Mark's amazing journey of personal tragedy and triumph gave him insights and attitudes that seemed to center his being. I liked Mark a lot and love him as a brother. Even to this day, Mark and I are in contact. He went on to become a big-time mucky muck executive at an international toy company and has beautiful kids (great gymnasts, go figure).

Micha made sure we were all introduced and then led us to dinner. The only place near our hotel just happened to be a Pizza Hut. So, that's where we went.

As a pizza lover, part of me was horrified at what I saw. In England, they put a couple of things on pizza that we don't in the states, including, eggs, peas, and tuna fish. We did not order that.

Each of us shared a little bit about where we were from. Leif and Micha were old friends by this time, so they had a rapport together. Mark and I were just excited to be there and felt like the rookies we were. Micha and Leif told us a little bit of what challenges to expect working in the suits. I had already done it on the first movie, so I had some idea of what was going on, but I wasn't used to all the electronics, or working with a puppeteer.

It was really nice to sit with these guys and connect for a bit. But soon, it was time to go. Leif and Micha were going to make their way to the West End, Mark went to a local pub, and I went back to the hotel and watched TV.

Man, was I lame.

TURTLE GAMES

T he next day we all met in the lobby in the morning and were driven to a high school gym. It was like the set from some English schoolboy movie in the 1920s. The gym was small and dusty, and filled with old fashioned equipment like wooden Indian Clubs, ladders and ropes, and an old-school pommel horse.

The puppeteers and a few technical folks were already there setting up their equipment. Micha and Leif greeted their counterparts with familiar affection. On this second film, Mak Wilson was again the puppeteer for Micha and Michelangelo; Rob Mills was taking over Leif and Donatello; Rob Tygner took over Mark and Leo; and David Greenaway was staying on as Raphael with me. I recognized David from the first movie, but this was our first time being introduced formally. David still seemed to me like a tortured artist, like a perpetually semi-drunk Keith Richards, or "Captain Jack Sparrow" from *Pirates of the Caribbean*.

Once we all shook hands and talked for a bit, the completed turtle heads were brought in. The technicians helped us strap on our computer backpacks and connect them to the heads. We slid them on and got used to the whole deal, moving around, adjusting the eye holes, just trying to get comfortable. The heads were heavy, weighing about 12 to 15 pounds. We each talked with our respective puppeteers through our headsets and ran through a series of tests. They made sure all the electronic connections worked and the communication headsets were functioning fine.

Once everything was deemed to be working, we went through some basic exercises to get our necks warmed up and used to supporting the weight of the head with all the motors. We looked to the left and right, tilting the head in various directions, making circles, etc. Then we started doing improvised movements with the puppeteers, moving in different ways, striking poses, and acting out different scenarios. The puppeteers wanted to see what facial expressions looked best in various situations and how they could best control them. It was all a feeling-out period, not only for us in the turtle heads, but for the relationships we were developing with our puppeteers, and for the technicians to take stock of the technological aspects. For this film, they had made some slight changes to the set-up of the remote-control systems and the wiring. This was the first opportunity to run them through the paces.

During improvisation exercises, the puppeteers were responsible for providing anything the turtles would say, and the actors were responsible for providing the hand and body movements to match. We could all hear each other because of the microphones and headsets mounted inside the helmets. Our puppeteers had the ability to control whether we heard everybody on an open channel, or if they hit a switch, they could make it a private conversation between puppeteer and turtle. We would listen to what lines our puppeteers delivered and react as best we could with body and head movements, whether acting surprised, sneaking around, or performing complete made-up scenes between the turtles. The puppeteers would carry on conversations, maybe let the characters argue, or even tell a joke, and we had to keep up and supply all the body language right along with them, including laughter, shock, fear, etc. It was a lot of fun. All of us actors were involved in movement-based arts in some way; Leif was a tumbler, Micha was a dancer, Mark was a gymnast, and I was a martial artist. Being challenged to communicate somebody else's spontaneous words

183

through accompanying movement was a joyful opportunity to use our skills.

The next day was a repeat of these same activities; trying on parts at the workshop and working with the puppeteers on improv, charades, and other activities. When the days were over, they would drive us back to the hotel and leave us on our own. Micha and Leif headed to the West End to hang out again. Mark went to a nearby pub and hung out with the locals again.

I went out for Indian food.

FRIENDS DO

Once I got back to North Carolina, things moved pretty quickly.

A college friend named Chris had just graduated and had been pursuing his own attempts at becoming an actor. He was doing local theater near Raleigh, NC and actually got a call to audition for *TMNT 2: The Secret of the Ooze*. He auditioned to play one of the thugs who attacks Keno the pizza boy in the shopping mall at the beginning of the film.

The producers were making Chris audition several times for a one-line part and he kept having to drive two hours down to Wilmington from Raleigh for all the call backs. A "call back" is when you've auditioned for something, and then, because they liked what you did, they call you back to audition again, this time in front of a director or producer who can make the final casting decision.

I called Pat Johnson, told him about my friendship with Chris and about how he was auditioning for the thug role. Since that role only worked for one day, I asked Pat if he would consider hiring Chris to be one of the Foot Soldiers so he could work on the film the entire time. Pat told me he would be present during the upcoming auditions and would keep an eye out for Chris. Ultimately, Chris went and read for Pat Johnson and was hired, not only to be a thug, but also as a Foot Soldier for the duration of the film. Needless to say, we were both super excited and Chris was going to be my roommate.

After talking with Leif and Micha in London, I knew some of the things I could ask for from the film's producers. For instance, instead of staying in the Holiday Inn with everybody else, I could request that the producers give me the weekly amount they were going to pay for my hotel room, and I could use that money to find my own place to stay. I called ahead and asked a local realtor to find a house directly on the beach that I could rent for the three months we were going to be working on the film. It turned out to be one of the best moves I could have made. I was 23 years old, playing one of the lead roles in a well-known movie franchise, and I was doing it all while staying in a beachfront house paid for by somebody else.

Winning!

APRIL'S FOOLS

A few days before we were supposed to head to Wilmington to start work, I got a call to come down just a bit early. The director, Michael Pressman, wanted to meet up and do some readings with the new "April O'Neil," Paige Turco.

I wasn't privy to the actual details or negotiations, but word on the street was that the original April, Judith Hoag, had been so outspoken about the treatment of the turtle actors and their terrible working conditions on the first movie, as well as negotiating for higher pay and credit on *Ooze*, that they did not end up bringing her back for the second film. I thought it was odd that they were going to use a totally different actress. But, I guess it's not the first time they've done that in Hollywood.

They were willing to pay me extra for the early trip down, so I jumped at the chance and drove the four hours to the studio. When I got there and met Paige, I immediately developed a schoolboy crush on her. She was so amazingly cute I couldn't stand it, and as a dancer, she had some of the greatest legs I'd ever seen. I was still very insecure when it came to dealing with women, so I managed to stutter out an introduction and shake her hand. She was very nice. Mark Caso was also there and he seemed to be much more in control of himself around her, calm in his yogi-like manner. We spent a little time with Michael acting out some of the scenes in the script, and he worked with Paige to try and find the right approach for her character's reaction to the turtles.

Paige was so sweet and excited to be part of the movie, she ended up taking us out for lunch on the docks by the beach.

STUNTS RULE

A few days later, everybody working on the film arrived in Wilmington, including my buddy Chris who joined me at the beach house. The other actor turtles took up residence in their various rental houses as well.

Starting work on the second film felt different than the first. I was honored, excited, and beside myself to be on the "first team" with the actors, director, etc. I was in the place that I had looked at and wished for just a year earlier.

Just like on the first film, we were going to start with a couple of weeks of rehearsal, while the crew built all the sets. During this time, I was reunited with Pat Johnson and many of the Foot Soldiers from the first film. It was great to see everybody again. I was also introduced to the new team of stunt turtles, all picked by Pat Johnson from the top competitors of the American karate tournament circuit. No longer were the producers going to employ stunt guys from Hong Kong, the language barrier and travel expense were too much. Now, with Pat Johnson's help, the producers figured out they could hire super-talented folks right in the states. The stunt guys were:

- Steven Ho–Donatello
- Larry Lam–Leonardo
- Nick Palma–Michelangelo
- Ho Sung Pak–Raphael

Also on the movie were some other stunt guys playing the giant monsters, Tokka and Rahzar. Kurt Bryant played Tokka and Mark Ginther played Rahzar. Kurt and Mark were tough Hollywood stunt guys that were friends of Tom DeWier. Mark Ginther seemed like a quiet family guy. He would go on years later to work as a stunt coordinator on bigger films, including *Solo: A Star Wars Story*. Kurt was a little bit more of a wild man and liked to have a good time. Tom DeWier knew that I liked to drink and he warned me, saying, "Hey Kenn, Kurt can go all day and night and be totally fine. Nobody can keep up with Kurt when it comes to drinking. Be careful." Being me, I took this as a challenge. Of course, I thought I could keep up with Kurt, I was an unstoppable superstar. I was currently living out my dream of being an action hero, and I had just completed four years of professional drinking training in college; I was ready for anything.

Yeah, right.

Eventually, drinking with Kurt would get me in a good deal of trouble; trouble that I had to lie to try and get out of, but still never escaped the consequences of. But, that comes later.

Being back on the lot and seeing all the fun that the stunt team was having getting together and working on fights with Pat and all the Foot Soldiers, I kind of missed being with them. Everything seemed so care-free for them. Guys playing the Foot, like Dale Frye and Johnny Holbrook brought a lot of fun and laughs to that crew, and Pat was the same stern but loving father figure that all the guys worshipped. It was obvious they were all having a good time. I immediately began to question whether I had made the right move striving for this new actor turtle position.

On top of all that, one of the most notable things that changed on this movie was the hiring of Terry Leonard, the new second unit director.

Terry was a stuntman, stunt coordinator, and director who is a Hollywood legend, and that's no exaggeration. He was going to be in charge of shooting all the action sequences and working with Pat Johnson to make sure all the fights were looking good. Terry's the real deal and I was lucky to get to know him on this film. He is as big as it gets in the stunt world. His name is kind of cowboy royalty left over from the pre-CGI days, when stuntmen were the toughest, craziest guys in the room, and there was nothing they wouldn't do for the camera. Terry had even met and worked with the godfather of all stuntmen, the famous Yakima Canutt on *Where Eagles Dare* in 1970 (when Canutt was 75 years of age). Canutt is considered the first "real" stuntman in Hollywood films and worked in a lot of silent films and old black and white Westerns as early as 1923. He's the guy who got dragged under the horses and wagon in the famous scene from *Stagecoach* starring John Wayne. What was exciting for me to discover was that Terry Leonard actually doubled for Indiana Jones in *Raiders of the Lost Ark* and plays Indy when he gets dragged under the truck, just like Canutt in *Stagecoach*. Terry also doubled Indy in the snake-filled tomb, when Indy knocks the large statue off its base, to break through the wall and escape. *Raiders* is one of my favorite movies of all time. I wanted to be Indiana Jones when I was a kid. I even bought a bullwhip and started practicing with it when I was young. I also bought a hat, but I looked like an idiot wearing it. Working with Terry was just like meeting a real Indiana Jones.

Terry was a real pleasure to be around on the movie set. I would even get to spend time with him after work at some informal gatherings in restaurants and bars. When Terry walked, he swayed back and forth in an exaggerated cartoon cowboy walk. I found out that he walked like that because both his hips had been replaced from the pounding they'd taken over the years. About his swaying gait, Terry said, "I walk like a drunk on roller-skates." Terry also liked tequila.

Terry was funny, talkative, and liked to tell stories. Lots of stories. As I got to know him, he would regale me and my buddy Chris with stories of things he did and people he knew in the wild days of '60s and '70s Hollywood. For one film, years earlier, Terry jumped off an eight-story building (80 feet) into cardboard boxes. Rather than landing flat on his back like he was supposed to, he accidentally hit feet first, causing his legs to buckle and his knee to slam up into his own chin, breaking his jaw and knocking himself out. He said he woke up in the hospital and the producer had given him a brand new Cadillac just to keep him happy.

Working his way up to be a top stunt coordinator in Hollywood had allowed Terry to transition into shooting action sequences as second unit director for some big films, including *Conan the Barbarian* and *Romancing the Stone*, two totally awesome movies... and *Blue Thunder*, I mean, c'mon!

I was drawn to Terry's spirit of action and adventure, just like all the action hero characters I had been drawn to as a kid. He was a real man, who did some real cool stuff.

JUMP AROUND! JUMP AROUND!

During the initial few days of rehearsal and pre-production, I would spend my time around the stunt guys and Foot Soldiers. The actor turtles, unlike the stunt team, were all busy doing their own private things on an individual basis and there wasn't that same "team" spirit that permeated Pat Johnson's action team. Micha was a bit older and doing whatever a bit older people did (not sure what that was at the time, but now I realize it's reading and going to bed early). Leif was busy living his own adventure, hanging out with a local girl he had met. And Mark was keeping his head down and lying low, just trying to do his best. I would come to find out later that this individualism was typical of actors in Hollywood.

Making it in the entertainment businesses is not necessarily a team sport. It's a business filled with individuals who all think they have what it takes to be the next big thing, and that doesn't really require or acknowledge anybody else in the process. Sure, you need directors and agents and others to believe in you and work with you, but these are just people who are exploiting actors because they think they can make money off of them. Once they don't think you can make any more money, they drop you like a hot potato. This is one of the reasons why it's so hard for relationships to work in Hollywood, because everybody's ultimately out for themselves. Over the years, I was like that, too. It's one of the reasons I eventually left Los Angeles, because I figured out I was becoming that which I didn't like.

Anyway, during this second film, I was still friends with many of the stunt guys and Foot Soldiers, so when we had time, we fell back into playing the Choi Da Di card game, as well as working out, and basically just hanging out.

One of the more fun things we got to do on this film when we had down time was practice high falls into big thick pads, like the kind Olympic high jumpers land on. There were a couple of these pads lying around the soundstage where the Foot Soldiers rehearsed and also some painters' scaffolds about 10-15 feet high. We would practice jumping and flipping off the scaffolds into the pads.

In addition to practicing our jumps, Chris and I could both do standing backflips. It was something we learned how to do while we were in college and could bust out on the dance floor after a few drinks. On set we used to challenge each other throughout the day to bust out a backflip at will. If I was walking by Chris, I would stop and say, "Are you an action hero?" and then he was required to do a standing back flip. He could also do the same thing to me. It got so some of the other Foot Soldiers got in on it and would say it to us as well, at any time, and Chris and I had to bust out a flip at a moment's notice.

Backflips give you great abs.

LET'S GET IT STARTED IN HERE

After the brief rehearsal period, the sets were all constructed and we got down to production time. The first thing we shot for Ooze was the shopping mall scene that opens the film. For the initial few days of the production, everything was focused on the stunt team and all the action sequences in the mall. It was very exciting to see the Ninja Turtles come back to life with all this breathtaking choreography. Everybody on the crew was understandably impressed by the amazing moves and athleticism of guys like Steven Ho (Donnie) and Ho Sung Pak (Raph). These guys were incredible martial artists and could do amazing jumps and kicks, even better than guys on the first film.

In addition to the fantastic new martial artists on the film, the action on *Secret of the Ooze* was slightly different than the first movie in a couple of ways. Because there was some blowback from parent groups on the first movie, believing the film was too violent for kids, the second movie had the following two declarations:

1. No turtle shall ever use their weapons.
2. When Foot Soldiers get knocked down, they must not lie still and appear dead, but rather, they must keep rolling around on the ground as if in substantial pain, yet very much alive.

195

The only time a single Ninja Turtle drew his weapon was in the very beginning of the movie, in the mall, when Leonardo draws his swords and throws them into the ceiling, so he can pull himself up and kick a bad guy in the face. Mikey does swing some sausages for nunchakus but never actually uses his own, and Donnie uses his staff once. Outside of that, no turtle ever uses a weapon. Many people never even realized that.

As for the Foot Soldiers never lying still after getting pummeled, during rehearsals and the shooting of scenes, Pat Johnson and the assistant directors were constantly standing on the sidelines shouting, "Keep moving!"

Those first few days were electric with action, but it was all action, and no acting. At this time, I was having more second thoughts about my new position on the film. I saw how much excitement was being generated by the stunt team, how much fun they were having, and how much attention they were getting. I thought maybe I had made a mistake climbing my way up to actor turtle status, after all. These guys seemed to be having the time of their lives and the crew was giddy with praise. I anticipated that the whole movie was going to be like this, and I was definitely jealous.

It turns out, it wasn't just me feeling all of this. All of us actors were starting to get a little anxious and feeling a little "left out" those first few days. Turns out, so was the director, Michael Pressman, as he ceded control to Terry Leonard to direct the initial action sequences. After a couple of days of this, Michael gathered us together for a turtle meeting.

"Hey, guys," he said, "I know it seems like we did all this work and intense preparation, and now that we're here, it's like we put the brakes on while they film the action scenes. I know it seems like everybody is excited about all the great work the stunt guys are doing. But, I want you to stay excited, too. Right now, everybody loves all the action, and they should because it's so good.

But, in a way, it's like the tail is wagging the dog right now. Just be patient for a bit, and we'll get a chance to do everything we've been working on."

I'm not sure if one of our guys had said something to Michael, but I guess as a good director, he was tuned in to what his performers were feeling and picked a perfect time to give us a pep talk. It seemed to work and we were all placated a bit.

TURTLE GREEN WITH ENVY

In that initial action sequence in the mall, the stunt guys handled the majority of the action, but each turtle had moments where they delivered dialogue in between the punches and kicks. For these moments, the actor turtles and puppeteers were brought to set and inserted into the appropriate moments. Each time one of the actor turtles was featured, Michael Pressman would assume directorial duties from Terry Leonard. One moment where Raphael has a line is when he grabs Keno the pizza boy during the fight and drops him in a trashcan to keep him out of harm's way. Keno was being played by Ernie Reyes, Jr.

As the stunt double for Donatello, Ernie had so impressed the producers on the first film with his talent and his pedigree that they wrote a part into the second movie, essentially so they could groom him for further movie stardom. You may recall that New Line Cinema, the company that distributed the original TMNT films, made *Surf Ninjas*, starring Ernie Reyes, Jr., Rob Schneider, and Leslie Nielson just a year later after *Ooze*. I was envious of Ernie, just like I was jealous of the turtle actors the year before. Sure, my dreams were coming true, I had gone from stunt turtle to actor turtle in less than a year, but Ernie had jumped a step further and gone straight from stunt turtle to onscreen movie star! Of course I wanted to be in his shoes! Who wouldn't? That was the whole idea, get to the point where you are an onscreen action hero, not hiding behind a rubber suit.

Ernie was kicking ass in the mall scene and demonstrating his awesome talents. Never mind that his amazing amount of previous experience and the fact that he had been kind of a celebrity his whole life contributed to his new opportunities, I was still green with envy. This kind of envy is what kept driving me from one level to another. I would see somebody doing something I wanted to do, and I would set my sights on figuring out how to get in that same position. Although envy is one of the seven deadly sins, I also believe it sometimes plays a role in spurring us on to new goals.

And now...a true turtle confession...

Today, I sometimes see Ernie at Comic Cons and I love him. When we see each other, we have a great time and spend a lot of time dining, drinking, and enjoying our weekends together. I enjoy his sense of humor and adventure. But, back when we were shooting the movie, Ernie and I weren't really close. We weren't enemies or anything, but I didn't care for, what I thought was, his attitude. Most of it can be attributed to the selfish jealousy that made me covet his good fortune, but part of it was also that I think Ernie acted big for his britches back then. He seemed to walk with a lot of swagger and what I interpreted as an entitled "celebrity" attitude. I can't say I wouldn't have been the same as him in those circumstances. In fact, I probably felt about him the way some of the Foot Soldiers felt about me on the second film. I was making selfish, personal judgements that I didn't think Ernie should be acting like he was, and there was nothing I could do about it. Except when it was time to film the opening scene.

In order for the turtles to protect Keno during the mall fight, the director wanted Raphael to wrap Ernie in a blanket, pick him up, and then drop him in a trash can, before exiting frame to rejoin the fight. When Michael called action, I said my line, threw a blanket over Ernie, hoisted him into the air, and then dropped him into the trashcan like a sack of rocks. I knew that Ernie couldn't see or control his movements while wrapped in the blanket, so he basically was at my mercy. We did several takes and Ernie got plopped down a few times. Nothing I did was really egregious, or overly violent, but it was fun to do it. It felt kind of cathartic. I could always blame any difficulties on the challenges of working in the suit.

And there were a lot of challenges working in the suit.

YES, IT WAS HOT

The single most frequently asked question I have gotten over the past three decades is, "Was it hot in that suit?" I've been asked this question so many times, that it's become a joke between me and my brother the doctor. I always ask him, "Is it hot being a doctor?"

Truth be told, it was hot as hell in those suits. You could lose 10 pounds a day in water weight just sweating. You'd immediately gain it back drinking Gatorade, orange juice, or water (like we did all day long), but you were basically wearing a sauna suit for six hours at a time. Our day would start early in the morning putting on our costumes. We would then work for six hours before breaking for lunch. During the break, we would remove the sweat saturated suits, take a shower, eat lunch, and then put on a separate, dry costume for the next six hours of the day.

At the end of one of those six-hour shifts, we could take off one of the turtle hands, which was like a long glove, and pour out the stream of sweat that had pooled inside. The only reason the sweat pooled is because the glove itself, and the entire costume, had already reached maximum sweat saturation, like a sponge that's full, or a Nerf football left in the rain. In one instance, in order to counterbalance the heat, they tried to devise some kind of cooling vest that could be worn under the suit, like something similar to what astronauts or fighter pilots might wear. Unfortunately, they didn't think about this until we were already in production, so it was too late to try and fit extra equipment under the form fitting suits. They tried stuffing these yellow plastic vests with tubes of water under our costume, but it only made the suits so tight you couldn't breathe, and they really didn't have the time or inclination to slow down production to try and figure out a more suitable alternative. They basically scrapped the idea and let us be hot.

Because the turtle suits were so hot and restrictive, there were some very real medical concerns about keeping the performers healthy and functioning. For this reason, the producers rented a separate, special trailer and parked it right outside the sound studio. The trailer had a kick-ass air conditioning system and they kept it cranked up, so at any time, the turtle performers could go outside and sit in the trailer to cool off. While this was a nice gesture by the producers, it was not very efficient. There was never enough time to actually leave the set and go sit in the trailer. It took so long to get outside of the soundstage and get situated that by the time we did, it was always time to come back to the set.

Because of this, Micha, the de facto leader of our turtle group, went to the producers and made a deal. He told them we would be willing to give up the cooling trailer, if they took the same amount of money they were paying to rent it and divided that money up among the turtle actors, so we could all rent cars to get around town. I had a motorcycle, but the other guys were all from out of town, so they had no transportation. Getting a car was great for each of them because it gave them freedom, and getting a car for me meant I didn't have to get stuck in the North Carolina rain anymore on my bike. The producers agreed and we all ended up driving little white Mitsubishis. Micha used to crack me up because every time he would climb into his cheap, little economy car, he would put on a set of Ray Ban aviator sunglasses and a pair of leather driving gloves like he was driving in LeMans.

Not only were the costumes ridiculously hot and constraining, but they were always breaking down and causing delays. The Henson folks would scramble like crazy to find a solution to whatever the current problem was, while the producers, Terry Morse and David Chan would fret over the time that was being lost.

As filming progressed on *Ooze*, we experienced lots of turtle breakdowns and the producers were becoming more and more concerned. Because of this, the puppeteers decided to play a trick on the producers.

The Henson group made a copy of Michelangelo's head and brought it to set as if it was the real one to be used in the scene. As the head rested on a stand, Michelangelo's puppeteer, Mak Wilson, acted as if he was having trouble getting the head to work. He became more and more visibly frustrated. After a few minutes of Mak ranting and raving, flipping his control switches back and forth to no avail, one of the technicians secretly set off a smoke bomb they had rigged in the head. The head looked like it blew a fuse. Mak, following through on his performance, screamed expletives in his English accent, yelled something about "Being tired of all this shite," picked up the Mikey head and threw it violently down into a pool of water that was serving as part of the dock scene for the end of the movie. The head hit the water with a splash and the producers watched slack-jawed as the main part of one of their $250,000 turtle suits sank into the murky depths. The crew held its collective breath waiting to see what would happen. At that moment, the producer David Chan from Golden Harvest saw through the ruse and let out with a big smile. He knew nobody would be stupid enough to do what Mak had just done…but the line producer, Terry Morse, just about had a heart attack.

203

LEGENDS ASSEMBLED

One of the great things about working on Ooze was the opportunity to meet and work with some pretty cool and notable folks.

Kevin Nash, a famous pro wrestler, played "Super Shredder." Super Shredder is the name of the Shredder after he drinks the ooze himself and morphs into a giant, muscle bound guy. For some reason, the ooze also seems to affect the Shredder's costume and makes it even bigger, badder, and more bladed than before (not really sure how the DNA-affecting ooze transformed his clothes).

Kevin was a very sweet guy, and huge. He also had a good sense of humor. Despite his massive size and intimidating look, the wardrobe department had some fun and made him some very feminine princess slippers to wear when he wasn't wearing his shredder boots; they were like a rich lady's bedroom slippers with pink sparkles and bows. He wore them with pride.

Kevin didn't like the fact that the Super Shredder costume had muscles painted on it. He felt like he had the build to carry it off, but eventually the producers convinced him it was for the best on camera.

When Kevin first started working with Pat Johnson and the stunt crew, he didn't quite understand how movie stunt fighting worked versus the way pro wrestlers did it, or if he did, he didn't give a shit. The first time he practiced choreography, one of the stunt guys threw a punch at Kevin and swung it in front of his face, missing by a few inches, just like you're supposed to do. Kevin didn't react, he just stood there.

Pat Johnson said, "Hey Kevin, I need you to snap your head to the side as if you've been hit."

Kevin responded, "Well, just go ahead and hit me, I'm used to it. I need you to hit me."

Pat smiled and explained that although that may be fine for wrestling, in movies we used camera angles and near misses to sell all the hits. Kevin wasn't a big fan of that. After so many years of full-contact professional wrestling, he wanted contact. Fortunately, he was a true professional and adjusted to Pat's way. I've since seen Kevin at a comic con or two and he is just as nice now as he was then.

Another true professional, and legend, working on the film, was the English actor David Warner. David was on the set playing "Professor Perry," the creator of the ooze. He was so cool. Although he'd been in a million things, to me he will always be "Evil" in Terry Gilliam's masterpiece film *Time Bandits*. I asked David about his experience with Terry Gilliam, the former member of Monty Python who, to this day, has films that represent some of the best directorial work I have ever seen, including *Brazil* and *The Adventures of Baron Munchausen*. David told me that Terry was like a child who saw incredible dreams and visions in his head and was able to translate them to the screen. We talked a little bit about the challenges David faced with the amazing body costume he had to wear in that movie to play Evil, but he was quick to point out that even though it was cumbersome, it could not compare with the torture that must be wearing a turtle suit with a full helmet and face covering.

David told me that he took the job in TMNT 2 because his grandchildren went crazy when they heard he was offered the part and would have killed him if he didn't take it. Despite being a Shakespearean actor with well-respected credentials, he was now hanging out in this cartoon-style film. He explained to me that British actors were different than American actors. According to him, British actors will work almost any job, in any medium, whether it be the stage, television or movies. Unlike American actors who, at the time, were traditionally either TV stars, movie stars, or Broadway stars, and who mostly stuck to whatever was their bread and butter, British actors try to work as much as possible and are thankful to have professional acting gigs, no matter how low on the totem pole they seemed. They very much realize they want to make money any way they can and consider it a blessing for anyone to hire them as professional actors. This is obviously the case for David Warner who has film and television credits that span from 1963 until the writing of this book in 2019. David would play a big part in helping the turtles when they had a showdown with the producers later on.

GO NINJA, GO NINJA, GO!

As much of a pleasure as it was to work with some of the talented people that worked on Ooze, other times it was not so pleasant. Not always because the people were unpleasant, but the circumstances were.

Since the first movie was such a success, the producers were able to parlay marketing and product placement deals for the second one. One of the deals they made concerned the nightclub scene that featured Vanilla Ice, aka Robbie Van Winkle.

The producers had a relationship with SBK Records, a record label known for progressive musical acts. At first, the record company pushed the producers to do a deal with the band Wilson Phillips, a very well-known trio of girls that sang a song called *Hold On*, a really big hit. But, the band didn't seem like a good fit with the sensibilities of the Teenage Mutant Ninja Turtles. The producers determined that SBK's other big star of the time, Vanilla Ice, would be a much more suitable fit for the film. His urban sensibility matched with the turtles more.

Vanilla Ice showed up on the movie lot with an entourage, backup dancers, and a lot of attitude. The producers bent over backwards to accommodate his every whim and take care of his gang. This kind of rankled all the turtle actors because we were pouring our sweat and blood into this movie and we could barely catch a break from the producers. As far as they were concerned, we were a handful of replaceable schmucks in rubber masks.

207

While Vanilla Ice was there, he celebrated his 21st or 22nd birthday and they threw him a party out on the backlot. There was a cake and candles, music playing through a sound system, and I remember somebody gave him a remote-control car. He spent a lot of time driving it around the parking lot and was proud to announce that he named it "Fuck."

That night, Vanilla Ice also taught me about his catch phrase, "Word to your mother." He used to say it at the end of his songs and also on stage and in interviews. At his party, I asked him what it meant.

He said, "You know, it's like "word" to your mother, for having you and shit. Respect to your mother." I thought that was a pretty cool sentiment.

When it came time to shoot the nightclub scene, and time to perform on stage, Vanilla Ice was supposed to lip sync the *Ninja Rap*, and the turtles, taking a moment to bask in the public eye, would get into the groove and perform a dance in front of the crowd. We had been working with a choreographer to all get the dance movements down for the past few days.

Once the nightclub set was filled with extras, the stage was filled with smoke, and we started shooting the scene. Unfortunately, Vanilla Ice didn't know the words to his own song and kept forgetting them! That sucked! Here we were, in those torturous turtle costumes, suffering and sweating every minute, dancing like trained monkeys in a sauna, and this guy kept screwing up the takes. We'd have to do them over and over again. It was a nightmare and it took forever. We had to repeatedly do the dance moves, with very little vision to see around us, and very little oxygen getting inside. We kept having issues, including dehydration and nosebleeds.

And on top of all that, I had a serious hangover.

I had been out drinking the night before with Kurt Bryant, the

stunt guy playing the snapping turtle Tokka. I did not heed Tom
DeWier's earlier warning about not being able to keep up with
Kurt's drinking. We were at one of the crew members houses
listening to Terry Leonard tell great stories and drinking tequila.
A lot of tequila.

I mean a lot of tequila.

The next morning, the day of the dancing scene, I felt like shit.
Even though I had taken my two *Goody's Headache Powders* (which
are the best hangover cure around), I was worn out and moving
slow. But, I knew I could rally.

I was wrong.

By the time we got through a couple of takes of the dance
scene, I felt like I was gonna be sick. I tried to play it off and told
Pat Johnson I wasn't feeling well, maybe I was coming down with
something. He said, "Kenn, I heard you were out drinking and
doing shots with Kurt last night. Seems like you might be hungover
this morning." He was calm, but I could tell he was angry. I was
angry too...apparently some shithead had ratted me out!

"Well, yeah," I said, "I had some drinks with Kurt, but I'm fine,
not hungover at all." Then, to prove my point, I banged my forehead hard with my fist several times. I almost passed out. "I'm just
feeling sick, like I've got the flu or something."

Pat raised his eyebrows and called the producer Terry Morse
over. "Kenn isn't feeling well, maybe sick. I think we should send
him to a doctor."

I looked up quickly...What? Send me to a doctor? Okay, this was
going further than I thought. Problem was, I couldn't stop my lie
without looking like a fool, so I agreed. At that point, they brought
in my stunt double, the amazing Ho Sung Pak, and he took over
for the rest of the dance scene.

I was driven to a nearby doctor and given a full work up.
This was like the days when I was a kid and got out of school by

pretending to be sick, either by spitting chewed up food into the toilet to look like vomit, or heating the thermometer on a lightbulb to make it seem like I had a fever. One time I even went so far that my mom took me to the doctor to get checked for an appendicitis. Back then I had also gotten myself too far into a lie and had no way out. I even kept up the charade as the doctor had his finger up my ass and was checking for internal issues. I am proud to say that, even with that finger squirming up my rectum, I never gave in. That's commitment. Just like then, this time on the set of the film, I was going to ride it all the way to the finish. To give in was to admit that I was hungover and that I had lied to Pat Johnson. No way was I going to do that.

Thankfully, after an examination of my symptoms and complaints, the doctor actually diagnosed me with some kind of a virus and reported it back to the producers. I now had a "legal" excuse and plausible deniability, but I don't think anybody was truly buying it. Like a politician, I refused to ever admit any wrong-doing...until now (I'm sorry, Pat).

When I got back to the set, nobody ever brought it up again, but I know that one of the producers filed the event away in his brain and when it came time to make the third turtle movie, he used this as ammunition to keep me out. Which is totally cool, because that movie sucked anyway.

FACE TIME

The nightclub scene stands out to me for another reason, as well. It was going to be my first real chance to get my face on the silver screen.

In the first turtle movie, you may remember, the actors who portrayed the turtles in the first film also appeared as human characters in small roles. Josh (Raph) was in the taxicab; Micha (Mikey) was a pizza delivery guy, David (Leo) was a gang member, and Leif (Donnie) was a Foot messenger. Now, in the second film, the other actors had once again negotiated for similar work. Micha makes an appearance as April O'Neil's downstairs neighbor; Leif had a speaking role as one of the Foot Soldiers; and Mark Caso (Leo) got to play a guy working in a TV newsroom alongside Michael Pressman (the director).

And then there was me.

I had briefly shown the back of my head in the video tape flop, *Dracula's Widow*, and I had been barely visible in the background of the Jay Leno/Pat Morita flop *Collision Course*, and even in the first turtle film, I was a guy behind a ninja mask or a turtle mask. So as of yet, you could never really see my face in a movie. Now, I had a chance for that to change.

Because I had no agent, I did not think to negotiate for this when I had to deal with negotiating my contract originally. But, after seeing the other guys perform some of their roles, I asked Terry Morse if there was something I could do outside of the costume and get some screen time myself.

"We'll find something for you," he said, and I was elated.

To his credit, the movie had already been cast, so it's not like there were acting jobs just waiting for me. What he decided to do was talk to the director and stick me in a non-speaking role (i.e., "extra") in which my job was to run into the nightclub for the opening shot of the Vanilla Ice scene.

For this particular shot, the camera started on me as I ran into the club and then followed me to the front of the stage to stare up and cheer on Vanilla Ice. When all was said and done, even though I didn't speak, my face would be plastered across the screen... pretty cool, I thought. Until I realized, many months later, the shot never even made it to the film; no sign of my face anywhere. It was kind of like what I felt about my "Talkative Foot #2" scene being cut from the first film, pretty disappointing. But, I was still a Ninja Turtle, so it all worked out okay.

TURTLE CON

A few days after the Vanilla Ice scene was done, and he and his crew were long gone, Leif passed out inside his suit. Or at least that's what the producers were supposed to think. Leif was upset with the way the producers were treating us compared to the way they had been treating Vanilla Ice and he wanted to get their attention. He actually warned the rest of us ahead of time that he was going to do this.

We were working hard, like we always did, sweating, straining, and sucking down bottled oxygen in-between takes. Then, after a significantly long take, Leif collapsed onto the floor. It was an unnatural fall, and totally not part of the scene, so immediately everybody knew something must be wrong. The crew rushed to his side, his dresser kneeling beside him and the set medic charging in. Leif was unresponsive.

They propped him up and immediately removed the head. Fortunately, Leif seemed to regain consciousness just as the head came off. At that moment, the director and producer put everything on hold and we took a break so they could make sure Leif was okay. Like a dutiful soldier, Leif contended that he could push on and get the shot...all for the good of the film.

As you can imagine, the producers weren't so concerned with Leif as a person, as much as they were probably concerned with what a death or hospitalization might mean to them both legally and financially. That was fine by the rest of us, we got a little bit of time to relax and Leif made a statement. I'm not sure if it affected anything that the producers did after that, but at least they were reminded that the turtle performers needed to be taken care of.

Years later, something Leif did would remind me of this moment.

When O.J. Simpson was getting ready to go on trial for double homicide, the media from around the world was in a feeding frenzy. Anything and everything having to do with O.J. was considered newsworthy. So, one day, I was watching the news and a tease came on for an upcoming story. The anchor looked into the camera and said, very dramatically, "A local resident is coming forward to say he saw suspicious characters around Nicole Brown Simpson's home just moments before the brutal murders were supposed to have taken place! Could this be a break in the case?"

Then they cut to a commercial.

Now, this was big stuff, especially for a population hungry for any revelations of new evidence in the murder case of the decade.

Of course, I was interested, too. I was fascinated by the whole O.J. thing. As a resident of L.A. I was familiar with the neighborhood where the crime had taken place and had been glued to the TV set for all the coverage.

Moments later, after the commercial break, the news came back on and segued right into the story. As they introduced the "local resident," I saw Leif Tilden pop up on the screen with his unique voice, talking about seeing some shadowy figures roaming around the area near the crime scene. They interviewed him, but his responses, and what he says he saw, were so vague that it really didn't have much value. I don't think anything came of Leif's claims after that, but as soon as I saw him on the TV that night, it seemed to me like he was pulling some kind of practical joke or performance art piece, injecting himself into one of the biggest news stories of the decade. I'm not saying he didn't see anything, but it reminded me what a good actor Leif was.

214

PHOTO OPS

Most of our days on this second film ran together in a blur of suits and sweat. We moved from set to set, including underground sewers, the new turtle lair in an old subway station, the construction site where the turtles face Tokka and Rahzar, and even a junkyard that was built both inside and outside. The outside set was used for the daytime scene when Raphael and Keno try to infiltrate the Foot Clan, and the interior was used for the night scenes when Raphael is held prisoner and his brothers come to save him.

The reason so much of the experience is a blur is because, as an actor, a great deal of the experience was all inside the rubber head. So, despite being in all these different environments, all we really ever saw was the inside of the head and the little bit you could see through the tiny eye holes. Sometimes we were inside the heads for an hour or two at a time with no break. On occasions like those, it was easy to become a bit testy.

One day we were on the set working and the well-known actors Laura Dern and John Heard were on the lot working on another movie called *Rambling Rose*. While we were shooting, the producers thought it would be a great idea if Laura and John wanted to come over and get their pictures taken with the turtles. I know that sounds cute, fun, and generous of the producers, but damn, we were sweating and straining. So, before they would let us take the turtle heads off to breathe from oxygen tanks, we had to stand around waiting for actors from another soundstage to walk over and snap some photos. I get it, this may not sound like a big deal, and I might sound like a whiny bitch, but talk to anyone that has to work in a space suit, deep dive gear, or even dress like a high school mascot, or a hamburger in front of a fast food joint, it's hot, hard work. With all the stress you're dealing with, the last thing you want to do is spend extra time in the suit for somebody else's pleasure.

During this film, as I experienced the working conditions, I began to develop a better understanding of why the original April O'Neil, Judith Hoag, had been so adamant about protecting and taking care of the actors in the suits on the first film.

WAY TO ROLL WITH IT, BARBARA

W e were grinding out our days and making our way through the film. When I wasn't being used on camera, I was spending time hanging out with my buddy Chris and around Pat Johnson's stunt team.

Like some of the other department heads, the producers had given Pat a golf cart to travel back and forth between the various soundstages. Chris and I decided to have some fun one day, so I asked Pat if I could use his golf cart to drive to the backlot and show Chris the city streets they had built back there. Pat agreed and we walked out the door and climbed in the cart. Just then, Pat's assistant Barbara stepped out and asked if she could come, too.

"Of course," Chris and I said together.

Chris jumped on the back of the cart and allowed Barbara to sit in the passenger seat next to me.

We drove to the backlot and I gave an impromptu tour of the facility. It was a lot of fun racing the cart around the backstreets with nobody else there. But soon, it was time to head back.

We made our way back towards the soundstage and, just as we were approaching, two things happened: I made a bad decision, and Pat Johnson stepped out of the door just in time to see me do it.

I was having fun driving the golf cart and decided I would try a *Dukes of Hazzard* style maneuver and surprise and impress my passengers. My goal was to go as fast as I could and, just as we got to the soundstage, I would whip the wheel 90 degrees to the left, hit the brake, and send the golf cart into a short sideways skid, coming to rest right by the door.

At least that's the way I saw it in my mind.

What really happened was, I accelerated, then just as we got to the soundstage, I whipped the wheel 90 degrees to the left, made the turn, and hit the brake. The golf cart did not go into a cool sideways skid like I envisioned. It just came to a sudden and complete stop... and Barbara was launched out of the cart and onto the pavement like she was shot from a catapult.

Barbara, who was probably in her late forties, maybe even fifty at the time, was very athletic and an accomplished martial artist, so she hit the ground and rolled with it pretty well. Unfortunately, Pat Johnson had just stepped out of the soundstage and watched the whole thing take place.

Luckily, Barbara was okay and actually laughed about it.

Pat did not laugh, and he never let me drive the golf cart again.

PARTY ON, DUDES!

If we had time off during the production, it might sometimes involve a trip to the local Hooters restaurant to drink and hang out with the waitresses.

One day, the assistant director told me that I was not on the call sheet for the next day and would not have to go to work. This is like being told you have a snow day at school. Like any experienced partier, I took my lack of obligation the next day as a license to get rocked that night. I'm talking beer and shots with my new friend... you guessed it...Kurt Bryant (Tokka). Like last time, I held my own pretty well, going shot for shot with Kurt. And like last time, I had a pretty severe hangover the next morning. I also made the mistake of having no drinking water in my rental house before I went to bed and I woke up parched.

I went for a walk on the beach to clear my head and go to the local store to pick up some hydration. It was beautiful outside and I walked about a mile to the store. By the time I got back, I was feeling much better and my phone was ringing. I ran inside and grabbed it.

"Hello," I said.

"Kenn, it's Jeff, the second AD. We've been calling you for a while. We need you to come to set!"

"But, I'm not on the call sheet," I said. "I'm not supposed to work today." My heart was beating fast. The last thing I needed was another Vanilla Ice hangover incident.

Jeff continued, "Yeah, but we're having trouble with the Michelangelo electronics and we're going to shoot Raph instead, so we need you here now. Do we need to send a car? We're waiting for you right now!"

"No," I said. "I'll get down there faster on my motorcycle." Then I hung up.

Shit!

When I got to set, the producer, Terry Morse started yelling at me that I should have been available. The reality was, he was wrong, because I was not scheduled to work, but I still looked like the bad guy because I held them up. Between that and the Vanilla Ice dancing hangover, I was not doing myself any favors in the producers' eyes. These things would all contribute to me not being invited back to work on the third film...but again, I'm okay with that...because the third film sucked.

It wasn't just alcohol that I got into during the film. One night, at the end of the shooting week, we were at the house of one of the crew members having a good time before our day off. As usual, I was having a great time drinking a little tequila and talking to Terry Leonard, listening to stories of the old stunt days. One of the other turtles pulled me aside and gave me a small, plastic film canister with a little bit of pot.

"Enjoy yourself, boychik" he said, then he hugged me.

The next day was our day off, so Chris and I stayed at the beach house, ordered a pizza, rented a VHS tape movie from Blockbuster, and proceeded to make a smoking device out of a two-liter Coke bottle, some tin foil, and a bit of tape. Then we smoked the shit out of that weed.

Now, I don't know if you, dear reader, know anything about smoking weed, but if you don't, let me tell you this...if you don't smoke pot, or don't smoke it a lot, it hits you pretty hard when you do, at least me. Unlike people who smoke it all the time and have a calm and controlled demeanor, if you're a rookie, smoking pot can send you into fits of laughter, paranoia, and hunger, just to name a few things. Well, that's what Chris and I were, rookie pot smokers. So, when we inhaled great billowing clouds from our homemade plastic bong, we got amazingly high. We didn't do anything nefarious or certifiably crazy, but I do remember a few things:

1. I kept turning somersaults all over the living room, rolling around like a gnome.
2. Chris could not stop laughing at my little rolling circus act and that only encouraged me to do it more, until I banged my head on the coffee table.
3. We ate a lot of pizza.
4. We tried to watch the movie *All Dogs Go To Heaven* on VHS and, for the life of me, I could not figure out what was happening in that movie. I kept having to stop the tape and ask Chris to explain it to me.

Fortunately, we made it through our day off and basically slept the rest of the night away. Chris was hooking up with one of the Hooters girls, so I think she might have come over. I went to bed alone and tried to figure out what that damn movie was about.

TURTLE DROP

When we went back to work, a serious accident took place. It happened during the scene in the junkyard when Raph is tied to a stake and his three brothers are coming to save him. As Leo, Mikey, and Donnie move towards Raph's position, they step into a trap set by the Shredder, and are swept up in a cargo net and lifted high off the ground.

To do this stunt, the crew constructed a large cargo net out of thick rope. The only problem was, when they scooped up the three guys in the loose net during rehearsal, it all bunched together and the guys stacked right on top of one another, like a giant teardrop. In order to avoid this, the crew welded together a large, square frame of metal pipe that would help the net retain a wider shape so that the turtles could be spread out along the bottom. Once this rig was all set up, the stunt guys practiced getting scooped up, the net being lifted by a hydraulic piston and pulley system. It worked great and everybody walked away, ready to film the scene the next day.

When the cast and crew came back to work the following morning, they prepared for the net scooping scene. Because my character was tied to the stake, I wasn't involved in this part of the scene and was elsewhere on the lot that day.

Nobody knew it, but overnight, the cable that was connected to the net, to lift it off the ground, had been touching and rubbing up against another metal cable, and the friction caused a breakdown in the fibers of the net cable. When it was time to film, and the director called "action," the stunt guys walked across the net and were hoisted into the air. When they got lifted up, about six or eight feet off the ground, the weakened cable snapped. The stunt guys were unable to see what was happening in their suits and dropped all the way to the ground with no way to protect themselves. It was a blind drop for these guys...and they hit hard.

Some minor injuries were sustained to backs and knees, but the guy who caught the worst part was Steven Ho, the double for Donatello. The heavy metal frame that the crew had welded together crashed down on Steven's foot...and CRUSHED it. I mean crushed it. He would later tell me that the doctors said his foot bones looked like a bowl of Corn Flakes.

Steven had to go to the hospital for emergency surgery and they patched together his whole foot. He was out of commission for the remainder of the movie. Fortunately, he would eventually make a full recovery. But, right after the accident, they had to bring in David Wald, a phenomenal martial artist, to finish out the show as Donnie.

WEARIN' OUT

At this point, the long, hard days on set, six days a week, had worn us all out. You could tell that everyone was feeling the grind of the shoot. I was feeling really lethargic, worn out from the ongoing cycle of hot, sweaty suit work 12 hours a day. But, I had to try and fight the feeling and get ready for an important moment in the film, "the backflip scene."

If you recall, at the end of *Ooze,* Splinter punishes the turtles by having them do backflips (although in the movie, they are back handsprings, not backflips), and for the last frame of the movie, the camera freezes on all the turtles launching themselves backwards. The first time, much earlier in the movie, Splinter told Michelangelo to do backflips and Mikey got caught cheating on them. Nick Palma, the stunt man playing Michelangelo performed these handsprings flawlessly. Now, for the end of the movie, in the final shot, all the turtles had to do one.

It turns out, the only stunt guy that could NOT do a back handspring was my double, the otherwise amazing Ho Sung Pak. Because of that, Pat Johnson approached me and asked if I could do the back handspring for the shot. In all honesty, I had never done a back handspring in my life, although I did know how to do a backflip. A back handspring was much more intimidating to me because you actually had to dive backwards, right towards the ground, leading with your head. If your hands missed, or your arms couldn't support the impact, you'd crash your noggin right

224

into the ground. Plus, trying to do it in a heavy, cumbersome turtle suit with a giant shell strapped to my back had me intimidated.

On the other side of all this fear, there was a chance for me to come out looking like a hero by stepping up to the plate and keeping the producers from having to hire another stunt performer to come in for the gag. It was a chance for me to maybe offset some of the missteps I had made earlier with hangover-affected performances. I just had to learn how to do a handspring and then practice it for the days leading up to the shoot. The problem was, I was so damn tired, the last thing I wanted to do when we had a break was go practice gymnastics. I needed some help.

Now, I have never been, and am still not, a coffee drinker. It's just never a habit I developed. But, as tired as I was then and with so much to do, I needed a way to kick myself into gear.

We broke for lunch one day and I headed up to the commissary to eat with Leif. He knew I was feeling worn out, he felt it too, and he told me that the commissary served great cappuccinos. At the time, I didn't know what a cappuccino really was, except it had something to do with coffee. Leif ordered one for me and one for him. I took my first sip.

It tasted really good, kind of like a chocolate shake with mocha flavor. It was so good, I drank it quickly.

Then I ordered a second one. And I drank that pretty quickly, too.

When lunch was over, we returned to set, strapped on our turtle heads and went right back to work.

And I bounced off the walls.

I couldn't stay still. Despite the exhaustion I was feeling earlier, now I was ready to dance the Ninja Rap, throw some karate kicks, and solve issues of world peace. I was talking incessantly with David, my puppeteer, through our headsets. I didn't realize at the time that I was doing anything out of the ordinary until David, in his droll English voice said, "Kenn, what have you done? You're like a rocket ship."

I told him about the cappuccinos at lunch and he said, "Ah, yes, that will do it." Then after a moment he said, "You should have one every day. I rather like this Kenn." For the next few days, I was hooked on the drinks and used them to fuel up for work and handspring practice.

Mark Caso, who had the experience of being an Olympic-level gymnast, gave me some great guidance on doing the back hand-spring. He had one of the other stunt guys get on his hands and knees behind me, and then I bent backwards, over that guy's back, learning how to target my hands to the floor. I did it first in regular clothes to get used to the movements. Then I did it with some turtle costume parts on, getting used to doing it with the added weight and encumbrance. Then I did it with the shell, which made it much more challenging to bend backwards. Finally, I did it with the head on. And since you can't see shit in one of those things, I just had to rely on muscle memory and basically do it blind. It was scary, but with Mark's help, I got it down pretty well.

At this time, I made another rookie mistake, probably the third strike that put me out of consideration for the third movie. I had been listening to Tom DeWier, Pat Johnson's favorite stuntman, as he gave me advice, or at least what I thought was advice. Tom told me to make sure that I asked the producers to give me a "stunt credit" in the film if I performed the back handspring. I wasn't exactly sure why that was important, but since Tom was telling me to do it, I figured I'd better follow through. He had a lot of experience and I was a neophyte actor who had no idea how the politics of the Hollywood system truly worked. Tom went on to explain that credits are what's important in Hollywood and how people judge you. He also said it would get me an additional paycheck for the day as a "stunt performer." I wasn't quite sure why a stunt credit would be so important since I was already getting the credit for being Raph the actor, but I didn't want to screw myself by not doing something I should, or missing out on a paycheck I might have justifiably deserved, so I decided to ask.

I nervously approached Terry Morse the producer and said, "I was wondering, because I'm going to do the backflip and everything, and that was supposed to be the stunt guy's job, well, I was hoping I could get a stunt credit for that as well."

He said, "What are you talking about?"

I could tell by his manner he was not fond of my request. I immediately became more nervous. "Well, I thought that since I was going to do the stunt work, that maybe I could also get the credit and the contract for it."

"Let me get back to you," he said and quickly walked away.

That at least gave me hope. Until I heard from Pat Johnson.

A little while later, Pat found me. "Kenn, my son, let's talk."

Terry had obviously gone and complained to Pat and Pat proceeded to explain to me that I wasn't doing myself any favors with my request and that it was out of line. I tried to explain why I had asked, and how Tom had told me what to do, but Pat wasn't having any of it. "Just do your job and be happy that you're here. You will not be getting another credit."

Dammit! I fucked up again. Based on my conversation with Tom, I wasn't sure what I had done wrong, but based on Pat's reaction, I knew it was something. I apologized and told him that I was confused. He let it slide, but damn, I was racking up the rookie mistakes.

In the long run, it all worked out. I stood alongside the other stunt guys and, when the director called "action," I popped a back handspring on camera, in full turtle regalia, right on cue. We did a few takes of it and we nailed it each time. I felt great about doing it and Pat told me I had done him proud by stepping up and doing it.

When you watch the end of the movie, the very last shot is a freeze frame on all the turtles, upside down, in mid-back handspring. It's a pretty cool shot. Unfortunately, my back hand-springs didn't look as good as they felt. When you look at that final frame, I'm the only one who's crooked and looks like he's about to fall over.

TURTLE WRAP

And that was it. We had shot the last frame of the movie. After all the trials and tribulations; the broken-down turtle parts; the stunt injuries; the hangovers, and the off-screen drama, we eventually got all of *TMNT 2: Secret of the Ooze* in the can. "In the can" is a term that comes from the days when movies were shot on film, just like this one was. Once you finished shooting a roll of film, you put the undeveloped film back in the metal film can, taped the edges closed to keep out light, and sent it off to the laboratory to be processed. When your entire movie was shot, and all the film rolls had been sent to be developed, your movie was said to be "in the can."

The whole movie was an incredible learning experience, a tremendous adventure, and the dream of a lifetime. Sure, I made some mistakes along the way, but I also learned a lot and gained insights into the business that would help me the rest of my career. I also made some great friends.

Mark Caso and I would go on to spend a lot of time together in Los Angeles after I moved there. Terry Leonard had actually become quite a good friend during the film and offered to help me in any way he could when I decided to move to L.A. Pat Johnson continued to be a mentor, eventually offering me jobs on other films and giving advice as I navigated my early career in Hollywood. I stayed in touch with Tom DeWier and we worked together on some projects years later.

Just like the first TMNT film, it was bittersweet for this film production to come to an end. It was a great sense of accomplishment to be finished, but it was also the end of a great time. It's amazing how close you get to a group of people that you work with six days a week for several months on something unique and intense as a film. When it's over, there's a great sadness, not only because you won't be seeing some of these people again, but because you also don't know what, if any, work is waiting for you around the corner. This can be exceptionally disconcerting when you're worried about how you're going to pay the rent.

Fortunately, there was one more thing we had to do that would help out in that regard...a lot.

It was a Barbara Walters interview.

BABA WAWA

As the last day of filming approached, the producers were presented with a fabulous opportunity. Barbara Walters, the famous television journalist, wanted to interview the turtles for her upcoming Academy Awards television special. She didn't want to interview the human actors, she wanted to interview the turtle characters themselves; Leo, Donnie, Mikey, and Raph.

Coincidentally, her special was going to air just a week or two before *Ooze* would actually open in theaters. If they let her do it, the producers would benefit from millions of dollars in free advertising just before opening weekend.

To get a Barbara Walters interview produced, it would require the actors in the mechanical suits, the puppeteers, and the Henson support crew, as well. The challenge for the producers was figuring out how to pay everybody so they could take advantage of the opportunity.

It's against Screen Actors Guild rules for producers to ask you to work on any production other than the one you were originally contracted for. For instance, if I am contracted to work on *TMNT 2: Secret of the Ooze* as Raphael, the producers cannot ask me to come to the set one day and act as Raphael for a Coca-Cola commercial. That would be them trying to get two jobs for the price of one. The producers would have to give me a separate contract with a separate paycheck to work on anything other than *Ooze* itself. Therefore, in order for the producers to accommodate filming the

Barbara Walters show, they had to wait until *Ooze* was completely in the can and the film production was officially over. Then, the very next day, they would hire us all to work one day for the interview, with a whole new contract, just for that day. A contract that, like all contracts, needed to be negotiated.

The unit production manager, Terry Morse, pulled each of us turtle actors aside privately and offered a full week's pay for the one-day shoot. We were each making anywhere from $1500-$2500 per week (maybe a little more for Micha and Leif). When Terry offered us a full week's pay for one day, Mark and I thought we had died and gone to heaven.

Then the actor David Warner paid us a visit.

David had heard about what was taking place and came to see the four of us at once. "Don't let them screw you," he said. "These producers are going to make so much money from the millions of dollars in free advertising they get from this show, they should pay you $20,000 each for the day."

My jaw hit the floor. I'm sure Mark's did, too. We were both happy with the week's pay, but David was making us aware we might be being taken advantage of.

David explained how we needed to stand up for ourselves. He hated to see actors treated unfairly. Then he left and let us talk amongst ourselves. During our discussion, we elected Micha to be our leader. He went back to Terry Morse and told him we would all do it...for $20,000 each.

Apparently, the reaction wasn't great. I wasn't there, but the story played out that the producer basically told Micha we could go screw ourselves. He told Micha they would hire the stunt guys to take our places to do it.

When Micha told us that, Mark and I just about shit our pants. We were gonna make at least an extra $2,000 for one day, and now nothing. That sucked.

As we continued to shoot the last few days of the movie, leading up to the interview special, I was sweating it out, thinking that I had lost a full week's pay. That money could really have helped me move to Los Angeles.

But, one thing we had in our favor was the nature of our relationships with our co-workers, specifically our puppeteers.

Each puppeteer and actor had spent the past few months, joined at the hip, six days a week, pretending to be the same character. A unique bond is formed doing that. And a unique loyalty.

The producers tried to follow through on their plan of having the stunt performers put on the costumes, but the Henson workers and the puppeteers proclaimed that it would not work. They would only work with the actors. The producers found themselves between a rock and a hard place.

I know the negotiations got a little heated, and the producers weren't happy, but at the end of the day, the producers came back to us with an offer! They couldn't afford to miss the opportunity, so they said they would agree to use us...and pay each of us $10,000 for the day!

What the hell?! $10,000 for a day's worth of work?

I was 22-years old! That was an incredible amount of money to me. I felt like my Hollywood dreams were coming true faster than I had even imagined.

Mark and I were walking around on cloud nine, just waiting for our big payday. And we didn't have to wait long.

The film wrapped, and most of the crew and cast either went home or were hanging around for a day until their flights left. Terry Leonard flew out, Pat Johnson left, and most of the other actors and stunt guys were gone. It was like an overnight ghost town.

233

The next day, Barbara Walters showed up with her small crew.

The production designers had set-up an area that looked like part of the turtles' underground lair, Barbara would interview the turtles there.

Just like in the film, the puppeteers were located off camera. They were the ones who would actually answer the questions that Barbara asked. We actors had to try and complement whatever they said, very much like the early improv exercises we did back in London for rehearsals.

All I knew of Barbara Walters was from her appearances on television shows like *20/20* and *60 Minutes*. She was a serious journalist. I also knew that comedienne Gilda Radner used to spoof her on the original *Saturday Night Live* as the character "Baba Wawa." I did not know what to expect of the real Barbara Walters as a person.

She turned out to be awesome. Her tone and manner were courteous and inviting. She struggled at the beginning, trying to understand how the whole process worked concerning the puppeteers answering from off camera, and also dealing with the sounds of the electric servos whining and squeaking underneath the masks. But, eventually she realized what she was dealing with and asked questions like the professional she was.

Then something happened that I will never, ever forget, and made me fall in love with Barbara Walters.

During the course of filming, we took a break from shooting and removed our turtle heads. Barbara could see how sweaty and exhausted we were and expressed her sympathy.

"My goodness," she said to me, "You look worn out."

I smiled and nodded. "It's okay. We're used to it."

Ms. Walters' assistant approached and told her she had a few minutes to eat some lunch and handed her a plain brown bag, like the kind kids take to school.

"Thank you," she said to her assistant.

I was amazed. Here was a million-dollar television personality, and she didn't demand a catered lunch or anything, just a simple brown bag lunch. She pulled out a sliced turkey sandwich wrapped in cellophane, just like any normal person would. I remember she very delicately unwrapped her sandwich. As she did so, she looked up.

She said to me, "Excuse me. You look so tired." And she held out her sandwich. "Would you like half my sandwich?"

That's when I fell in love with Barbara Walters. She was offering me half her lunch and it was so incredibly sweet. I did not take it but smiled and thanked her deeply.

Years later Barbara Walters would say that interviewing the Ninja Turtles was the dumbest thing she ever did.

DREAMS DO COME TRUE

It was done!

The movie was over, the Barbara Walters special was complete, I had some money in my pocket, and I was ready to return to Greensboro on top of the world, determined to take the next step on my action-hero journey and get to Hollywood.

In just over a year, I had gone from an unknown, unemployed, action-hero wanna-be, college student, to playing one of the most popular characters in martial arts movie history, "starring" in a highly anticipated sequel...and putting money in the bank to boot. Everything was working out in my favor. Sure, I screwed up a few things along the way, but I've come to learn that's part of the journey, no matter what you're doing. You just have to keep moving and overcome the next challenge.

I thought back to when I first got picked on in school by Chase Woolen and decided to take karate. It seemed such a long time ago, but everything was still so vivid in my mind.

I remembered the pain of long sessions of karate training, the joys of competing, and the feeling that I could do anything I wanted. I felt totally unstoppable, able to achieve any dream I wanted, and there was nobody that could tell me differently. And that had proven true.

I gathered what few possessions I had, sold my motorcycle to one of the other Foot Soldiers and caught a ride back to Greensboro with my buddy Chris. Our plan was to spend the approaching

Christmas holiday with our families and then head out to Los Angeles to break into Hollywood together. My buddies Steve and Tony had already moved out from North Carolina about six months before, just before we started filming *Ooze*; so they were already scoping out the city, had found a place to live, and were learning their way around.

For me, it only seemed like I had to take the next step of moving to Los Angeles to keep marching towards my goal. I felt confident because I was well on my way, everything was working out for me, and I hadn't even left my backyard of North Carolina yet.

I felt like much of what I had learned as a martial artist had brought me to where I was. I had been determined to reach my goal, and no matter how hard it got, just like the intensity of training, the heartbreak of competing, and the pain of getting punched in the face, I never gave up.

Now, I wanted to launch myself to the next level in style, so I bought a first class, one-way ticket to Los Angeles. It was very symbolic for me. I felt like I was moving to the next phase of my life, I expected great things, and I would not be returning. When I got to L.A., I would buy a car with my Barbara Walters money, put *Teenage Mutant Ninja Turtles I & II* at the top of my resume, and begin my conquest of the action film industry, making my way to being the next action hero.

It wasn't until I actually landed in Los Angeles, caught up with my friends, and crashed in their tiny, roach-infested apartment in the heart of Hollywood that reality would settle in.

But, that's another story.

(And it ends with me starring in a karate movie and beating Al Pacino at the box office!)

Who dat baby?

We are family!

Bring on the bad guys!

Becoming a man.

239

Kiai!

A fellow 'chucker, ay?

My first headshot.

Homemade ninja outfit!

College party shape.

Action hero shape.

Graduating in 4 years with a 2.3
GPA and a 4.0 in partying!

Extra work on "Collision Course"
playing a drug dealer.

Pat Johnson and his Foot Clan.

At the beach with stunt guys from Hong Kong
and my roommate Steve (orange trunks).

Working out with Pat Johnson and Foot Soldiers.

Practicing high falls.

Choi Dai Di

Putting on fire protection
suits for the burning antique
store; me and Paul Beahm

Discussing action with Ernie while he gets in costume. See the head connected by wires to the computer pack worn under the shell.

Me crashing through April's skylight

It fits!

Working out the choreography

Yes, it's hot in that suit.

*In the subway with Pat Johnson. The
published photo that got me in trouble.*

Halftime in Arizona!

*Me and Ric Meyers, AKA Wade Barker, writer
and author of "Ninja Master" books.*

Getting my body cast made.

Me and my bulging body.

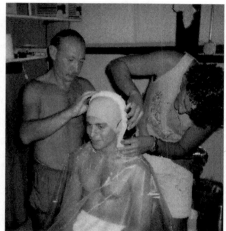

Getting my head cast made

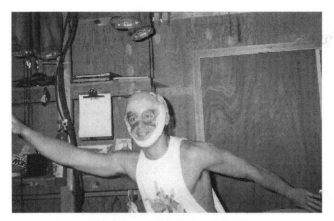

This helmet holds the turtle head.

See my eyes?

Red body cast for Raph.

Turtle parts hung up to dry.

254

A day in the junkyard.

Hungover during the "Ninja Rap" dance.

The four turtle-teers!

Crane stance!

256

Cast & crew photo from "Secret of the Ooze."

Barbara Walters interview.

*Me, Leif, Mark, and Micha at
the premiere of TMNT II.*

*A drawing given to me by Kevin
Eastman, co-creator of TMNT.*

Kenn Scott was born in New York, grew up in North Carolina, and chased his dreams to Hollywood, California. With a lifelong desire to be a movie action hero, Kenn trained in martial arts, acted in the theater, and studied film production, until all the work paid off and he found himself playing "Raphael" in the original Teenage Mutant Ninja Turtles films of the early 1990s. After that, working as a Hollywood stuntman and actor, Kenn appeared and starred in other films, including the martial arts cult hit SHOWDOWN, and then moved behind the camera to write and direct for movies, television, and even the CIA! Today Kenn is creative director of an advertising agency in Fort Worth, TX and still loves to travel, meet friends, and visit with turtle fans all over the world.